IN PURSUIT OF HAPPINESS

BOSTON UNIVERSITY STUDIES IN
PHILOSOPHY AND RELIGION

General Editor: Leroy S. Rouner

Vol. 16

In Pursuit of Happiness

Edited by
Leroy S. Rouner

UNIVERSITY OF NOTRE DAME PRESS
Notre Dame, Indiana

Library of Congress Cataloging-in-Publication Data

In pursuit of happiness/edited by Leroy S. Rouner.
    p. cm. — (Boston University studies in philosophy
and religion; v. 16)
   Includes index.
   ISBN 0-268-01174-5 (alk. paper)
   1. Happiness.   I. Rouner, Leory S.   II. Series.
BJ1481.I5   1995
170   dc20   95-16518
                                           CIP

∞ *The paper used in this publication meets the minimum requirements*
of the American National Standard for Information Sciences—Permanence of Paper
for Printed Library Materials, ANSI Z39.48-1984.

Manufactured in the United States of America

For John Silber,

presidential participant in several of our Institute programs, and long-time supporter of the interdisciplinary conversation which our program represents. His Institute lecture was a carefully crafted analysis of the roots of morality in religious sensibility, and his vision for the University in troubled times has reaffirmed those values which have made Western culture a noble tradition.

Contents

Preface

Boston University Studies in Philosophy and Religion is a joint project of the Boston University Institute for Philosophy and Religion and the University of Notre Dame Press. The essays in each annual volume are edited from the previous year's lecture program and invited papers of the Boston University Institute. The Director of the Institute, who is also the Editor of these Studies, chooses a theme and invites participants to lecture at Boston University in the course of the academic year. The Editor then selects and edits the essays to be included in the volume. Dr. Barbara Darling-Smith, Assistant Director of the Institute, regularly copy edits the essays and prepares the manuscript for the Press. We are currently working on Volume 17, *The Longing for Home*.

The Boston University Institute for Philosophy and Religion was begun informally in 1970 under the leadership of Professor Peter Bertocci of the Department of Philosophy, with the cooperation of Dean Walter Muelder of the School of Theology, Professor James Purvis, Chair of the Department of Religion, and Professor Marx Wartofsky, Chair of the Department of Philosophy. Professor Bertocci was concerned to institutionalize one of the most creative features of Boston Personalism, its interdisciplinary approach to fundamental issues of human life. When Professor Leroy S. Rouner became Director in 1975 the Institute became a Center of the Boston University Graduate School. Every effort was made to continue that vision of an ecumenical and interdisciplinary forum.

Within the University the Institute is committed to open interchange on fundamental issues in philosophy and religious study which transcend the narrow specializations of academic curricula. We seek to counter those trends in higher education which emphasize technical

ix

expertise in a "multi-versity," and gradually transform undergraduate liberal arts education into preprofessional training.

Our programs are open to the general public, and are regularly broadcast on WBUR-FM, Boston University's National Public Radio affiliate. Outside the University we seek to recover the public tradition of philosophical discourse which was a lively part of American intellectual life in the early years of this century before the professionalization of both philosophy and religious reflection made these two disciplines topics virtually unavailable even to an educated public. This commitment to a public tradition in American intellectual life has important stylistic implications. At a time when too much academic writing is incomprehensible, or irrelevant, or both, our goal is to present readable essays by acknowledged authorities on critical human issues.

Acknowledgments

Our first debt is to our authors, whose expertise makes this volume possible. In a number of cases they have made extensive improvements on their original lecture texts, and for this we are very grateful.

The person who does the hardest work on the manuscript is the Institute's Assistant Director, Dr. Barbara Darling-Smith. I invite the lecturers, edit their texts, and decide which ones to use, and in what order. Then I write the Introduction. But this is the fun part. The lengthy and exacting work of copy editing, which is not so much fun, is all hers, and her capacity for accurate detail is legendary. The mysteries of umlauts, diacritical marks, Sanskrit spellings, and the dark, complex truths hidden deep in *The Chicago Manual of Style* have all been revealed to her. And while copy editing may not be fun, working with her always is. She makes sure we get it right, and have a good time in the process. This year she has had expert help from Mark Lazenby who has entered Barbara's corrections to the text on the computer, presided over the scanner, and added his own wry observations to the process. Syd Smith also provided invaluable last-minute assistance.

Ann Rice, Executive Editor at the University of Notre Dame Press, oversees production of each volume. Since we have to choose a date for our annual publication party well before we begin manuscript preparation, we count on Ann's quiet authority to keep us on schedule and make sure we have the books in time for the party. And behind it all is our friend Jim Langford, Director of the University of Notre Dame Press, who was willing to take a chance on a series which most publishers would not have risked.

Finally, a final salute to our friends at the Lilly Endowment. At a time when the Institute lacked funding, Craig Dykstra, Vice President for Religion, and Jeanne Knoerle, S.P., Program Director for Religion, decided to support us with a three-year grant. Like our publisher, these good friends have also become colleagues and participants in our program planning, and their intellectual and spiritual support has been invaluable.

Contributors

CHARLES L. GRISWOLD, JR., is Professor of Philosophy and Chairman of the Department of Philosophy at Boston University. He is the author of *Self-Knowledge in Plato's* Phaedrus; *Platonic Writings and Platonic Readings;* and the forthcoming *Liberalism, Virtue Ethics, and Moral Psychology: Adam Smith's Stoic Modernity*. He received his M.A. and Ph.D. from Pennsylvania State University.

MICHAEL FISHBANE is Nathan Cummings Professor of Jewish Studies at the University of Chicago. He is author of *The Kiss of God: Mystical Death and Dying in Judaism; The Midrashic Imagination: Studies in Hebrew Exegesis;* and *Garments of Torah: Essays in Biblical Hermeneutics*, among other books and countless articles and reviews. A Guggenheim Fellow, he received his Ph.D. from Brandeis University.

JAMES R. LANGFORD is Director of the University of Notre Dame Press. Educated by the Dominicans, he received graduate degrees in both philosophy and theology at the Aquinas Institute. He is the author of *Galileo, Science, and the Church*, and, given that writing about baseball is his hobby, he has written four books about his favorite team, the Chicago Cubs. He and his wife are cofounders of THERE ARE CHILDREN HERE, a non-profit corporation dedicated to nurturing disadvantaged children.

MARGARET R. MILES is Bussey Professor of Historical Theology at Harvard Divinity School. Among her numerous publications are *Desire and Delight: A New Reading of Augustine's* Confessions; *Carnal Knowing: Female Nakedness and Religious Meaning in the Christian West*; and *Practicing Christianity: Critical*

Perspectives for an Embodied Spirituality. She received her Ph.D. from the Graduate Theological Union, Berkeley.

LEROY S. ROUNER is Professor of Philosophy, Religion, and Philosophical Theology; Director of the Institute for Philosophy and Religion; and Director of Graduate Studies, Department of Philosophy at Boston University. He is General Editor of Boston University Studies in Philosophy and Religion and has also edited *Philosophy, Religion, and the Coming World Civilization* and *The Wisdom of Ernest Hocking* (with John Howie) and *Corporations and the Common Good* (with Robert Dickie). He is the author of *Within Human Experience*; *The Long Way Home* (a memoir); and *To Be At Home: Christianity, Civil Religion, and World Community*.

HUSTON SMITH is Thomas J. Watson Professor of Religion and Distinguished Adjunct Professor of Philosophy Emeritus at Syracuse University. For the past three years he has served as Visiting Professor of Religious Studies at the University of California, Berkeley. His book *The World's Religions* (formerly *The Religions of Man*) has been for thirty years the most widely used textbook for courses in world religions and has sold over 1.5 million copies. He is also the author of such books as *Beyond the Post-Modern Mind*; *Essays on World Religion*; *Forgotten Truth*; and (with David Griffin) *Primordial Truth and Postmodern Theology*.

RUTH L. SMITH received her Ph.D. in social ethics at Boston University, where she was a Roothbert Fellow. She also holds an M.T.S. in ethics and theology from Harvard Divinity School, an M.A. in linguistics from Ohio University, and a B.A. in literature and music from East Tennessee State University. She is Associate Professor of Religion in the Humanities and Arts Department at Worcester Polytechnic Institute. Professor Smith serves as consultant to the Global Village Documentary Film Company and is currently working on her second project with them, a Public Broadcasting Service film on the sexuality and moral identity of teenagers. She is the author of numerous articles, and her essay in this volume reflects her continuing work on the moral implications of liberal thinking and their relation to contemporary feminist construction.

WILLIAM M. SULLIVAN is Professor of Philosophy at La Salle University. The author of numerous articles, he is (with Robert Bellah, Richard Madsen, Steve Tipton, and Ann Swidler) author of the three books *Habits of the Heart: Individualism and Commitment in American Life*; its companion volume *Individualism and Commitment in American Life: Readings on the Themes of Habits of the Heart*; and the subsequent work *The Good Society*. His latest work is *Work and Integrity: The Crisis and Promise of Professionalism in America*.

ROBERT A. F. THURMAN is Jey Tsong Khapa Professor of Indo-Tibetan Buddist Studies and Chair of the Department of Religion at Columbia University. He is author of *The Politics of Enlightenment*; *The Tibetan Book of the Dead: The Natural Liberation Through Understanding in the Between*; *MindScience* (with Daniel Goleman); and (with M. Rhie) *Wisdom and Compassion: The Sacred Art of Tibet*. With a B.A. and an M.A. from Harvard University, he completed his Ph.D. from Harvard in Sanskrit and Indian Studies.

TU WEI-MING is Professor of Chinese History and Philosophy at Harvard University. He has also taught at Princeton University and the University of California, Berkeley. He is the author of *Neo-Confucian Thought: Wang-ming's Youth*; *Centrality and Commonality*; *Humanity and Self-Cultivation*; *Confucian Thought: Selfhood as Creative Transformation*; and *Way, Learning, and Politics: Essays on the Confucian Intellectual*. He is a fellow of the American Academy of Arts and Sciences.

Introduction
LEROY S. ROUNER

HAPPINESS IS A PARADOXICAL THING. In our heart of hearts we all want to be happy, but we don't talk much about it, lest we seem sentimental, or too optimistic. These are difficult times for most, and tragic times for many, so we tend to harbor a faint hopelessness about the future. There is even a quiet cynicism about the possibility of happiness which is now fashionable, even among those who would seem to have every reason to be happy. But these quaverings in the face of the future will surely sabotage that element of spiritual robustness which the good life requires. Hence this inquiry into the nature of happiness, exploring the bold hope that the yearning in our heart of hearts may not be entirely unrealistic after all.

But what would happiness be like, if we could find it? Underlying the reflections which follow are several running arguments. One of the most notable is between those who hold that happiness is a form of tranquillity, rest, or peace found in the present; and those who hold that, while happiness is present to us, it comes primarily as anticipation, a desire which is yet to be fulfilled. Our first section confronts this argument head-on, with essays on tranquillity, desire, and blessedness.

Charles Griswold notes that philosophers in the Western tradition have had relatively little to say about happiness in spite of its enormous importance to human life. After a brief survey of that literature he turns to his own definition of happiness as tranquillity. He emphasizes that he means happiness in the long term, not some momentary experience. And tranquillity is not some static emptiness. It is indeed more like rest than motion, and it is an end state, but it differs from contentment. Happiness is tranquillity in the sense of "reflective integration over time." In this sense happiness has overcome any deep anxiety in one's life which would lead one to doubt "the fittingness of one's basic stance." This is not to deny the turbulence

1

attending one's many passions, attachments, and commitments; it is only to undergird this turbulence with the tranquil assurance "that basically one would change nothing in one's life" and that one is fundamentally at peace with oneself.

Griswold distinguishes his view from that of Epictetus, who argued that the loss of a child need not provoke any emotional response if one's inwardness is tranquil. Griswold, on the other hand, admits that one would suffer tremendous grief, but that one's essential tranquillity would not be shaken "for I will still say that it was right and good that I had this child." He is not making the extreme claim that one could still be happy while being tortured on the rack, but he turns to Socrates as an example of tranquillity within our grasp even in the midst of great misfortune. This is different from contentment, as Griswold sees it, not only because contentment is momentary but because it is "a state of mind severed from an appraisal of the truth of the matter." Hence contentment and unreflectiveness are natural allies, and Griswold's tranquillity is both reflective and related to what the ancients knew as a life of virtue. It is this "reflective arrangement of one's life" which quells any deep anxiety about what sort of life is worth living, and makes tranquillity the definition of happiness.

Margaret Miles has a different view. She is concerned to emphasize the role of the body in human happiness, and she turns to Augustine for an understanding of happiness as desire. For Plato and Aristotle happiness was the fruit of a rationality attainable in this life. With the noted qualifications, this is also Griswold's view. Augustine, on the other hand, regarded happiness as fulfilled only with the promised resurrection of the body in the life of the world to come. In this life we have only glimpses of ultimate happiness. Miles has many arguments with Augustine, but in this context she notes approvingly that Augustine was the first to insist that happiness is not purely spiritual or rational and cannot occur until the body is rescued from mortality and vulnerability.

Perhaps even more to the point for Miles is Augustine's break with that classical tradition which regards happiness as a form of tranquillity. For Augustine, happiness is "perpetually and irreducibly in motion," a form of desire as "a matter of survival, the act of self-identification of the hungry heart." The soul, he said, is shaped by the objects of its habitual attention and affection, i.e., by its desire and delight. To love the world as though it could provide permanent fulfillment is soul-destroying, because the objects and people in our experience are fragile and fleeting. The soul survives only by attaching itself to God, a "totally trustworthy object" which cannot die. But we know something of ultimate happiness through our experience of joy in this world. Here Augustine is refreshingly realistic; "base joys and disgraceful things" are as joyful as "good and worthy joys," and all provide a glimpse of what it will be like "where true joy is to be found" in our final reunion with God.

Happiness in this life is precious precisely because it is part of a dynamic process, and is therefore both fragile and fleeting. Here Augustine replaces the classical Greek emphasis on rationality with a characteristically Christian emphasis on feeling and will, even though reason remains, for him, the highest single capacity of human beings. In stating her own view of happiness Miles joins Augustine's view of life as a dynamic process of desire and delight with Plotinus' notion of the interconnectedness of all things. She affirms a universe "interwoven through veins of energy and delight" and "a faith in the immense generosity of the universe, experienced as beauty."

Both Griswold and Miles conclude with notions of happiness which focus on a particular interpretation of human experience, and are not dependent on the reality of any transcendent metaphysical realm. Huston Smith's reflections on blessedness, on the other hand, come to a specifically religious conclusion about "an additional level of reality . . . that houses a Being who in ways is distinct from us and is concerned for us." He begins with a philosophical analysis of human experience, much in the manner of Griswold and Miles, but he concludes with a move which neither of them make, a theological affirmation about transcendence.

He begins with the observation that happiness is a polar concept, paired with its opposite, unhappiness; and that human life oscillates between these two poles. But blessedness or beatitude is not subject to what Miles has so felicitously called the "fragile and fleeting" character of ordinary human happiness. Smith rejects the idea that happiness is pleasure, since pleasure derives from the the bodily senses. Here the distinction between Smith's and Miles' analyses begins to take shape. Smith does, however, share Miles' view that happiness is a phenomenon which characterizes the self in relationship. "Joy" is not quite what he means by blessedness, either, for joy is a sensation which surges through us when we are doing especially well at what we are good at doing, whether it be intellectuals excited by new ideas, or children "who with astonishing dexterity turn Double Dutch Jump Rope into a new art form."

Blessedness, for Smith, is not fragile and fleeting, but it is paradoxical. He turns to the Beatitudes in the Gospel of Matthew, noting that six of them are paradoxical; the poor, the sorrowful, the insignificant, the hungry and thirsty, the reviled, and the persecuted are all somehow "blessed." Some of these blessings are cast in the future tense; the sorrowful, meek, hungry, and reviled are blessed now because later they *will* be comforted, or they *will* inherit the earth. But two other Beatitudes are self-contained. For the poor in spirit, and those who are persecuted for righteousness' sake, "theirs *is* the kingdom of heaven."

Smith concludes that reason dead-ends in paradox when considering the ultimate nature of human happiness as blessedness. At this point philosophical reason "is an inadequate instrument for discerning Reality, the way things finally are." Smith turns to William James' comment about the religious experience of the mystics, for whom "contradictoriness and conflict . . . were melted into unity." So Smith defines blessedness as a paradox in which the nobler of the opposites absorbs the other. The result is an experience which shares some elements of what Griswold means by tranquillity, but is both transcendent and paradoxical—the "peace which passes all understanding."

Our second section deals with happiness in three major world religious traditions: Judaism, Buddhism, and Confucianism. We begin with Michael Fishbane's essay on "The Inwardness of Joy in Jewish Spirituality." His aim is to articulate the dynamic tensions between law and spirit, the natural and the supernatural, in which the Jewish sense of spiritual joy is generated. He notes the famous passage in the *Mishna Torah*, in which Moses Maimonides makes it clear that "a joyful performance of the commandments is an exalted form of worship and expression of the love of God." Maimonides cautions that such joy should not be for self-aggrandizement, but should be selfless in humility before God. "In this way, the wholly natural emotion of joy is transformed through divine service and actualizes the religious love which must motivate the worshipper." This joy has theurgical power; it leads to the divine indwelling in the worshipper, and transforms the spirit.

Fishbane then turns to the sixteenth-century literature of Jewish spirituality in which the transforming power of joy in the life of the worshipper is stressed, as over against the older ascetic practices and ideals. Especially notable are such mystics as Rabbi Eliezer Azikri and Rabbi Elijah de Vidas. In his *Reshith Hokhmah* de Vidas interprets Psalm 148 as "nothing less than the praise of the Cosmic Pleroma, or intra-divine structure." And the secret of the psalm, as de Vidas reads it, is that this divine structure is ultimately "a concordance of joyful song." The result, for the worshipper, is the joyful service of God.

The joy of spiritual inwardness in the Jewish mystical tradition is a kind of celebratory ecstasy which is tied closely to the performance of the law. In Fishbane's analysis joy is the dynamic power which related law to spirit, the divine to the human. Robert Thurman's essay on "The Buddha's Smile" presents a different interpretation of religious happiness. Fishbane's mystical joy is intense and weighty religious business. The smile with which the Buddha received enlightenment, on the other hand, is almost light-hearted. Thurman describes it as "a cheerful smile," and his thesis is that enlightenment *is* happiness in the Buddhist tradition. Further, "all beings are equal in that all are naturally concerned with the pursuit of happiness." And, for Buddhism, the secret of one's own happiness is selfless altruistic concern for the happiness of others.

Thurman is well aware that the popular view of Buddhism is one of morbid pessimism and nihilism. He suggests that the corollary of the thesis "enlightenment is happiness" is that "ignorance is misery," and the Buddhist tradition, in stressing the miseries of ignorance, has seemed pessimistic. For Thurman, however, this is realism, not pessimism, as he stresses in referring to the famous four Noble Truths as "Holy Facts." He cautions, however, that they are "facts" only for the enlightened. "Ordinary egocentric individuals" regard their occasional human happiness as real happiness, whereas the Buddha argued that "relative happiness is just punctuation in the rhythm of suffering; but fortunately there is an absolute happiness that is greater, deeper, secure, and ultimately blissful." Thurman provides numerous textual examples of the "orgasmic bliss" which is the "universal passion . . . the ultimate expression of universal compassion transforming to universal love, energized by inexhaustible bliss."

The texture of happiness in the Confucian Way is as different from the Buddha's cheerful smile as it is from the intense inwardness of Jewish mysticism. The Confucian view of happiness, as Tu Wei-ming presents it, is more complex than the unified bliss of the Buddha, or the integrating spiritual joy of the Jewish worshipper. Tu notes that "the fundamental concern of the Confucian tradition is learning to be human." Happiness is the satisfaction derived from gaining one's humanity. It is more complicated than happiness in either the Jewish or Buddhist traditions because both of these tend to be individual-istic, in spite of the emphasis on fulfillment of the law in the Jewish community, and compassion for all beings in the Buddhist release from ignorance and suffering. In Confucianism the human seeks har-mony with nature and with Heaven, acknowledging the intercon-nectedness of all those ways which define the human condition.

If Buddhism seems pessimistic about life, Confucianism is quite the contrary. One of its defining characteristics, Tu tells us, is faith in the creative transformation of our human condition "as a communal act and as a dialogical response to Heaven." The community is a necessary vehicle for human flourishing. The idea of an individual as sepa-rate from the community is unthinkable in the Confucian tradition. "Through an ever-expanding network of relationships encompassing the family, community, nation, world, and beyond, the Confucian seeks to realize humanity in its all-embracing fullness. This process of inclu-sion helps deepen our self-knowledge at the same time through a ceaseless effort to make our body healthy, our mind-and-heart alert, our soul pure, and our spirit brilliant. Self-cultivation is an end in itself and its primary purpose is self-realization." But the self which is real-ized is a social self, a citizen of a cosmic community. To realize oneself in that context is what it means for the Confucian to be happy.

Our third section deals less with definitions of happiness than it does with various issues regarding the meaning and even the uses of happiness. My own essay is an exploration of the thesis that ecstasy, the ultimate form of human happiness, is the necessary context for a certain type of knowledge. In making that argument I am going against the grain of a long-standing distinction between scientific and religious ways of knowing, based on the differing objects of knowl-edge (nature and God), the way that knowledge is received (reason and revelation), and the kind of language used to express it (philoso-phy and theology). My two test cases are from Aristotle and and the contemporary philosophical theologian, Paul Tillich. Aristotle, as scientist, asks how we can know that the first principles of any science are true, since—like the principle of plane geometry that the shortest distance between two points is a straight line—they cannot be proven. They are like the rules of a game, except that game rules are arbitrary, and scientific first principles must be true.

The analogous question in Tillich's theology is how we know that the first principle of theology—the reality of God—is true. Aristotle appeals to a nonrational (but not irrational) intuition in order to establish the truth of the *archai* of science. Tillich, it seems to me, is more interesting and thorough in his analysis of that intuitive experience as an exercise of "ecstatic reason." There is a moment in which the self "stands outside itself" (the literal meaning of "*ex-stasis*") and, without losing contact with itself, is momentarily available for contact with the transcendent. For Aristotle the "unmixed and separable" *nous* (or "world reason") is "divine" in that it conjoins the intelligibility of our minds with the intelligibility of the Cosmic *Nous* itself. Tillich is more specific in showing how that conjoining is set in the necessary context of "ecstatic reason," and how that same context is the vehicle for knowledge of the reality of God.

Next we turn to Ruth Smith's dialogue with her mentor, Reinhold Niebuhr, exploring the relationship between happiness and what Niebuhr called "the uneasy conscience." Make no mistake; in Niebuhr's vocabulary an uneasy conscience is a good thing, as opposed to the too-easy conscience of modern liberalism, which joins the Confucians in its belief in the creative transformation of human life. And while Niebuhr is no Buddhist, he agrees that modern liberals are ignorant about their own true condition, and that their sense of happiness is ephemeral. Smith is concerned with the relation between happiness and moral experience and reflection. For Niebuhr the events of the twentieth century—the Holocaust, the Great Depression, two World Wars, Stalinism—were enough to distinguish between the liberal view of happiness and his own view of morality.

Smith has a good deal of sympathy for Niebuhr's Christian realism, but she also has disagreements, especially with Niebuhr's individualism, which frames the moral life as homeless in this world, alienated by the necessity of participating in its power, yet resigned to doing so. She points out, however, that Niebuhr was really quite at home in the world of power, and *liked* being an influential person. She concludes: "Surely, as adults we can make some distinctions with confidence between well-being and sloppy contentment so that we do not teach others to fear and disvalue the world—even as we try again and again to make the world a place in which those most vulnerable can enjoy less fear and more value."

William Sullivan's issue is the meaning of professional life, and the possibility of happiness inherent in the promise of professionalism. One particularly troubling element in modern professional life is the so-called "yuppie syndrome." For this analysis, two features of professional life are significant. One of them is the freedom to employ one's human capital to maximum advantage and personal satisfaction. But this strains against the second feature, which is dependence on a demanding collective enterprise. The yuppie syndrome is a situation where public and private purposes have become increasingly disjointed. "The yuppie confounds much of our conventional cultural wisdom. . . . The yuppie both works very ambitiously and has an insatiable appetite for the consumption of stimulating commodities and experiences. The problem of yuppie life is rather that both success and pleasure seem . . . not only precarious but ultimately capricious and vain."

But Sullivan is still hopeful that professionalism will recover its moral bearings. "Professionalism, as a form of civic life, can give moral significance to the instrumental functions of work in ways which allow its participants to control and take responsibility for their actions as free persons." Professional life is institutional life, and Sullivan notes that "institutions . . . are tangible bearers of meaning, carriers of causes, vehicles of common life." He argues that the institutional patterns in which we live and the practices which they support are the major source of meaning, and therefore happiness, in our lives.

We conclude with Jim Langford's nostalgic reflection on the long-ago rivalry between the Cubs and the Red Sox. If the cheerful smile of the Buddha can provide a light-hearted balance to the weighty intensity of various mystical ecstasies, then a little philosophical playfulness would seem a not inappropriate way to end our excursus into the pursuit of happiness. Jim is a scholar of some note, but he loves baseball and the Cubs, and the happiness theme was too good an opportunity for him to turn down. So he gives us a little Aristotle, and a little good Catholic theology, but mostly he gives us hilarious stories about "the game," its characters, its drama, and the way it makes a true baseball fan genuinely happy. Oh, to be at Wrigley, on a summer afternoon, when the Cubs are there. . . .

All of which reminds us that the point of reflecting on happiness is to learn how to be happy, and perhaps to remind us that we are luckier than we realize. At the least, we all have brief moments of joy. And we all have the reflective opportunity, which Charles Griswold celebrates, for a rationally ordered life in which we take responsibility for our choices, and have the satisfaction of trust that we have chosen well. Those of us who are religious have had moments of God-given ecstasy; and, most important of all, we know something of Huston Smith's deep assurance that nothing in heaven or earth can finally separate us from the love of God, and that we are therefore truly among the blessed.

And even for those who are not religious, but who are sensitive to the life of the world around them, there is still what Margaret Miles has called the Great Beauty, the realization that the world in its benign generosity can be lovely beyond any singing of it. In these times of tragedy and trouble, that alone is enough to give us an Augustinian "glimpse" of what it means to be truly happy.

PART I

Tranquillity, Desire, Blessedness

Happiness, Tranquillity, and Philosophy

CHARLES L. GRISWOLD, JR.

> The happiness of mankind, as well as of all other rational
> creatures, seems to have been the original purpose in-
> tended by the Author of nature, when he brought them
> into existence.
>
> —Adam Smith[1]

FEW QUESTIONS POSSESS as great an existential urgency, and general philosophical interest, as "what is happiness?" If happiness is not *the* ultimate end of our activities, as Aristotle argued, it is certainly *an* ultimate end. A life without happiness seems scarcely worth the having. The "pursuit of happiness," in Jefferson's Lockean phrase, seems thoroughly woven into all our projects and aspirations.

The topic nonetheless possesses several strange features. The first is that philosophers have had relatively little to say about it in spite of its enormous importance to human life. One would have thought it an indispensable topic for a Platonic dialogue; yet no Platonic dialogue is devoted to it. Aristotle and some of his Hellenistic descendants did, of course, write on the subject. But they are the exceptions that prove the rule. There exist some limited treatments by major Christian and medieval philosophers; one thinks of the remarks by Boethius in *The Consolation of Philosophy* and by Thomas in the *Summa Theologiae*. But no major medieval treatise devoted to the subject has come down to us. Descartes, Spinoza, Locke, Leibniz, Berkeley, Voltaire, Hutcheson, Hume, Burke, and Smith offer us remarks, but once again no extended treatment. Diderot ruminates on the subject, and in *Les Reveries du promeneur solitaire* Rousseau offers us something more like a meditation than an argument. Kant has relatively little to say about the nature of happiness, even though happiness plays a major role in the architectonic of his ethical system. For Hegel, too, the topic is of derivative interest.[2] Husserl, Heidegger, and Sartre have precious little

13

to say; Nietzsche's remarks are scattered; surprisingly, there are no long treatments in Emerson, Thoreau, James, or Dewey. Among the classical utilitarians, only Sidgwick makes extensive remarks, but these scarcely amount to a comprehensive treatment of the subject.[3] We have Bertrand Russell's essay,[4] a few scattered remarks by Wittgenstein, nothing by Whitehead of note. There exist contemporary discussions and no doubt there are other pieces one might mention.[5] My point is that by and large the major philosophers in the Western tradition have not paid the topic a great deal of attention.[6]

This leads me to a second observation about this subject. Nonphilosophers seem generally to assume that there is an answer to the question "what is happiness?" Some claim to have found it and (perhaps for a fee) will tell you how to do the same. At the same time, there seems to be general agreement that happiness *is* a hard thing to "find," that is, to define and to attain. It is a strange situation; happiness is so much a part of us as to be unable to remain unknown; yet we cannot find it.

A third observation is that "happiness" is used in many ways. It can be spoken of as contentment, or tranquillity, or blessedness, or ecstasy, or as a mood, or as well-being, to name a few. One could speak of it in the long-term or in the short-term sense. We are not always clear about which sense we have in mind when we talk casually about our being "happy." Our vocabulary of happiness is not a fail-safe guide to the meaning of the term.

In identifying a sense of what happiness can mean, however, one must appeal to some intuition or opinion, and inevitably others will appeal to other intuitions and opinions.[7] We must, as Aristotle says, start with what is known to us in order to reach what is knowable in itself (*Nicomachean Ethics* 1.4.1095b2–7). But parts of what is known to us conflict with other parts.

This problem is implicit in prephilosophic ordinary intuitions. People often assume that happiness has a "you'll know it when you see it" quality. Yet people also recognize that they frequently see mistakenly; they will say "I thought he was so happy! I've known him for years! I can't believe he committed suicide!" Or again, people often associate the accumulation of wealth with happiness, and perhaps are motivated to accumulate wealth precisely because they think it will bring them great happiness. Yet moralists have always told us, and experience seems to confirm, that neither the pursuit of wealth nor success in that pursuit bring happiness.[8] So we must recognize that there are conflicts between prephilosophical intuitions about happiness. I see no way of avoiding this old methodological problem, though I do not infer that the problem is fatal to any effort to reach more than parochial conclusions.[9]

In approaching the notion of happiness, I have one particular sense of the term in mind, namely that in which we can speak of a person as generally "happy," as happy over the long term. In my long-range sense of "happiness," you could say you are happy even though at the moment of saying it you might not feel happy. We often feel happiness at this or that object; for example, I can be happy when I receive tenure. But this is different from the happiness that applies to a life as a whole and which thus arises from a certain way of leading a life. In choosing to reflect on happiness in this more comprehensive sense, I am following Aristotle's lead. You recall his remark that "one swallow does not make a spring, nor does one sunny day; similarly, one day or a short time does not make a man blessed (*makarion*) and happy (*eudaimon*)."[10] Kant too, for all of his differences with Aristotle, speaks of "happiness" in this long-range sense (see note 6 above). I thus mean to distinguish happiness from joy, ecstasy, a romantic transcending bliss, and the like. Happiness, in the sense I am discussing it, is not a mood. These may perhaps be referred to legitimately by our word "happiness," but I am interested in discussing this other sense of the term, because it is precisely this sense which people seem most to have in mind when engaged in the pursuit of happiness.

"Happiness" has both subjective and objective qualities; it is both an experience and a notion, and neither of these two dimensions should be ignored. Calling such and such the conditions of happiness is to have a view of this rather than that experience of which these are the conditions. At the same time, first-person reports of one's experience can be mistaken. As I reflect on what I mean when I say my life is or is not happy, I see that I have judgments in mind about myself, the world, what is satisfying now and over the long term, what is worth pursuing and avoiding, and so forth. I could be mistaken in assessing any of these things.

I shall argue that the experience of happiness is best understood, *ab initio*, in terms of tranquillity. At the same time, I shall suggest that we cannot be happy unless we rightly assess the conditions of our happiness. I shall attempt to elucidate what happiness is by distinguishing it from what I shall call "contentment," and shall explore further the connection between happiness and assessment or reflection. One needs a right understanding of happiness in order to be happy. Then I will attempt to understand the relationship between happiness and a particular kind of reflection, namely, philosophy. Like Epictetus, I think it crucial to explain why a Socrates can be happy even when faced with execution, and the explanation involves the relation between philosophy and happiness. I shall argue that the sort of account Epictetus gives of this remarkable phenomenon is, however, incomplete at best.

My argument resembles that of ancient ethical theories in that it connects happiness with virtue (or excellence of character), virtue with reflection, and reflection with philosophy. I am also incorporating the more modern view that happiness should be described as, in part, a feeling or experience of a certain sort.

Needless to say, there are many other issues that a comprehensive treatment of the subject would have to cover, including a discussion of what constitutes a well-ordered life. I cannot here offer any such comprehensive treatment. In the course of my rough sketch of this subtly textured landscape, I have adhered to Aristotle's injunction that one should expect only so much precision as the subject matter allows, and I trust the reader will do the same.

I. HAPPINESS AND TRANQUILLITY

> Happiness consists in tranquillity and enjoyment. Without tranquillity there can be no enjoyment; and where there is perfect tranquillity there is scarce any thing which is not capable of amusing.
>
> —Adam Smith[11]

Happiness is best characterized in terms of tranquillity. So understood it captures the connection between happiness and being at rest. Happiness is more like rest than motion, in two senses. First, in the sense of lacking significant discord; it is peaceful, at a deep level. Second, it is more like coming to a stop rather than like a process of moving towards a goal. Happiness resembles an end state, a completion or fulfillment, rather than a condition of lacking and overcoming of lack.[12] For this reason, happiness and contentment seem alike, and later I will say more about the difference between the two. When one says "I have lived happily" or "I am deeply happy" one means, among other things, that one does not experience significant internal discord, and that fundamentally one occupies a spiritual place from which one does not desire to move. One is not, at a deep level, anxious; basically, one is properly oriented, and one's fundamental stance towards the world is complete, at rest. I am sketching, as a starting point, this sort of view of the experience of happiness.

"Tranquillity" usually translates the Greek term *ataraxia*, a term that is the natural competitor to *eudaimonia*, which is the one that Plato and Aristotle use. The latter is normally translated, with trepidation, as "happiness," and less often as "blessedness"; *ataraxia* is also difficult to translate, and "tranquillity" is something of an approximation. "Imperturbability" also captures something of its sense.

The word *ataraxia* does not occur in Plato and Aristotle. It is to be found in important passages in Sextus Empiricus, Epictetus, Marcus Aurelius, and Epicurus, among others. The alpha privative is not, of course, captured by "tranquillity," and this is one way in which the translation is imperfect.[13] In its verbal form, with or without the alpha privative, the word goes back to Homer. There it is used of horses, among other things; a horse struck by an arrow "disturbed" (ἐτάραξε) the chariot and other horses (*Iliad* 8.86); "Taraxippus" ("Disturber of Horses") spooked race courses. In a number of writers the verb can refer to mental or physical personal disturbance, or to the "disturbance" of a polis, that is, the upsetting of civic discord, since stirring up trouble, agitating, distracting, leads to loss of *ataraxia* in the community. One can "disturb" a thing, as when one stirs up a body of water; a mud-slinger or muck-raker can "disturb" an individual or community; one can "disturb" in the sense of meddle, upset; an army or navy that is thrown into confusion is thus described by Thucydides. At 4.96.3 Thucydides uses the verb in describing a battle in which Athenians mistakenly kill one another as a result of their general confusion and disorientation.

In general, then, peacefulness and calmness (ἡσυχία) are akin to *ataraxia*. Understood as *ataraxia*, happiness is a state of mind, or better, a state of soul. In speaking of *eudaimonia*, Epictetus explicitly equates it with *ataraxia*, with freedom and absence of passions (*apatheia*).[14] It is rather like a state of peacefulness, being in control, inner harmony, calm, rest; as opposed to a state of war, desiring that which is out of one's control to obtain, internal discord, disturbance, motion, perturbation. But I do not want to endorse this Stoic view in its entirety, not just because similar views about happiness as *ataraxia* are to be found in the Sceptics and Epicureans, but also because there are problems with it. Let me elucidate the direction of my argument by means of several passages from Hobbes.

In Part I of Hobbes' *Leviathan*, we read: "*Continuall successe* in obtaining those things which a man from time to time desireth, that is to say, continuall prospering, is that men call FELICITY; I mean the Felicity of this life. For there is no such thing as perpetuall Tranquillity of mind, while we live here; because Life it selfe is but Motion, and can never be without Desire, nor without Feare, no more than without Sense."[15] Further on in the book Hobbes takes up the same theme. After declaring that there is no such thing as a summum bonum, contrary to the "books of the old Morall Philosophers," he states: "felicity is a continuall progresse of the desire, from one object to another; the attaining of the former, being still but the way to the later. . . . And therefore the voluntary actions, and inclinations of all men, tend, not only to the procuring, but also to the assuring of a contented life. . . . I put for a generall inclination of all mankind, a perpetuall and restlesse desire of Power after power, that ceaseth onely in Death."[16] Life is, in other words, continually in motion because ceaselessly driven by desire, anxiety, and fear, and fundamentally, the fear of violent death. Human life is fundamentally disturbance, disquiet, or ταραχή. From this anxiety or motion Hobbes explains a wide range of human phenomena, from competition to conscience, to ambition to curiosity to eloquence.

If life were like this, in motion and anxious, then we surely would not call it happy; we would not possess what Hobbes calls "perpetuall Tranquillity of mind." Hobbes seems right in associating contentment with the movement from one satisfaction to the next; it seems intrinsically unstable even though it seeks stability. The operative contrast in Hobbes' picture, then, is between "felicity"—or what we might, taking our cue from his own words, better call repeated "contentment"—and tranquillity over time. Felicity is inseparably interwoven with anxiety, whereas tranquillity is not. We can accept that some lives, that of the tyrant for example, lack even felicity; Xenophon's *Hiero* provides a wonderful discussion to that effect, and helps us understand why the notion of the "happy tyrant" is oxymoronic.

Hobbes' parallel distinctions between felicity and tranquillity, motion and rest, desiring and completion, seem basically right. But we need not accept the view that happiness has been completely described in this manner, or that it is impossible in this life.

On this view, the enemy of tranquillity is anxiety. I have in mind not so much anxiety about this or that event, but rather a general anxiety about things being out of kilter, not stable, not holding, potentially dissolving.[17] When Hobbes talks about the fear people have that their competitors might gain enough power to threaten them, he is getting at the latter, though he remains within the sphere of the political. That nagging doubt, or even the quiet dread of . . . of what? Perhaps it is something like dread that the foundations on which we built our life are not yet finished, or may crumble, or never were well laid. Perhaps (we think silently to ourselves) my life has been a waste, amounted to nothing. What have I become? What will become of me? Was this a praiseworthy life? Even worse, the soul may whisper to itself: "I don't know, things are so difficult to discern clearly, I seem surrounded by grayness and beyond that by darkness, everything is so . . . indefinite, formless." When questions such as these eat away your soul, anxiety or ταραχή has won out over happiness (cf. Adam Smith, TMS 6.2.3.2., p. 235).

Ataraxia captures what one might call the affective, subjective dimension of happiness. And that feeling or experience or state of mind is, speaking in broad terms once again, something like a sense of basic tranquillity, restfulness, peacefulness.

The association of happiness with tranquillity is a very old one, and seems to me to articulate one fundamental view of the matter. A competing view follows Aristotle in associating happiness with activity (*energeia*). The debate between Stoics and Aristotelians, in other words, articulates basic alternatives. Aristotelians define happiness as activity of the soul in accordance with excellence (*arete*). There is a place, if a problematic one, for "external goods" in this picture; happiness is not just the exercise of virtue. This is what one might call an objectivist definition of happiness, and it has several obvious advantages. It provides us with a means of assessing claims to happiness and of explaining how people can be mistaken in thinking they are happy. It links up happiness with ethics and with how one leads one's life as a whole. It provides a basis for distinguishing between happiness and contentment.

Putting aside problems of making sense of the notions of soul, natural function, and excellence, and the famous difficulty of reconciling practical and theoretical virtue, however, this definition does not link up clearly with the experience of happiness.[18] Aristotle says that excellence (*arete*) is not a *pathos* (*Nicomachean Ethics* 2.5.1105b27), and never says that happiness is a feeling (a *pathos*).[19] Since happiness is *energeia*, its activity would seem at odds with the passivity connoted by the term *pathos*. And as an activity in accordance with virtues that by definition are not feelings, it would be strange if happiness were understood by him as a feeling or emotion. His word for happiness (*eudaimonia*), and his association of happiness with human flourishing, lead him to think of happiness as a condition of self rather than an experience.

But, surely, the happy life is something someone actually experiences. Could the proper functioning of soul be compatible with a life of unsettled anxiety? Could one be happy in Aristotle's sense but not be aware that one is happy? About the closest Aristotle gets to a sustained discussion of the experience is in the analysis of pleasure in Book I, 8, of pleasure and friendship in Book IX, 9 (he notes for example that friends help the good man become aware of his own existence as something good), and of pleasure and theoretical virtue in Book X of the *Ethics*. He does grant that a life of misery and pain (such as that of Priam) cannot be happy. Yet this remains distant from some view of what it feels like to be happy. Aristotle's reticence on the subject leaves open the objection that he has analyzed not happiness so much as the conditions for being ethical, and further that one could be ethical in his sense but, affectively speaking, be unhappy.[20] It is hard to see how Aristotle would link up tranquillity with activity of the soul in accordance with virtue, especially because that activity indisputably requires, on his account, moral virtue. Can the tumultuous life of the courageous statesman or soldier be happy in the sense of "tranquil," on Aristotle's view?

And there is a second difficulty with the Aristotelian view of happiness. He views happiness as activity, not simply in the actualization of potentiality but in specific actions; the telos consists in actions or activities (*Nicomachean Ethics* 1.7.1098b15–20). Happiness is being at work in accordance with excellence. For Aristotle it cannot be characterized as *kinesis* because *energeia* is not a movement from a beginning point to some telos: it is the actualization of that telos.

Kinesis ceases when it reaches its telos; *energeia* does not. Yet *eudaimonia* is not simply lack of movement either; it is the kind of spiritual or intellectual motion engaged in when we philosophize or listen to music.[21] One could be moved by those experiences, or undergo them as one would painful work. Insofar as this view lacks a place for the notion that happiness is rest and peacefulness, it strikes me as at the very least incomplete.

But neither of the two basic alternative views of happiness—the Aristotelian and the Stoic—is alone adequate. In spite of my endorsement of the association of happiness with tranquillity, however, one cannot accept that association without qualification. There are two main reasons for this.

First, it would be easy to infer that felt tranquillity is real tranquillity. But I take it that our account must preserve the possibility of self-deception or failure of self-knowledge; and therefore that, as already indicated, our account of happiness requires something like an objectivist view of the sort Aristotle articulates.

Second, the tranquillity view of happiness tends to be associated with *apatheia*, with passionlessness, detachment, or indifference. Yet to live a life of tranquillity so understood rightly strikes us as barren, dry, uninspired. To eliminate psychic motion altogether, and then to call the resulting tranquillity "happiness" seems to purchase happiness at the price of human fulfillment, serenity at the price of our humanity. Why should we accept a notion of happiness that demands so high a price? Epictetus tells us: "Never say about anything, 'I have lost it,' but only 'I have given it back.' Is your child dead? It has been given back. Is your wife dead? She has been given back."[22] Or again, Epictetus recommends that we react to the death of our child or wife just as we would to another man's loss of his child or wife.[23] Happiness is to be ἀπαθῆ, ἀτάραχον, to have one's own affairs under one's control.[24] How shall I free myself from disturbance, asks Epictetus' interlocutor: "Have you not heard over and over again that you ought to eradicate desire utterly, direct your aversion towards the things that lie within the sphere of choice, and these things only, that you ought to give up everything, your body, your property, your reputation, your books, turmoil, office, freedom from office?"[25] To be passionate is to be moved, sometimes by things that are not under our control; at one level, then, passion is the price of *ataraxia*, precisely as Epictetus argues. In the final analysis, this view of tranquillity is so extreme as to provoke a Nietzschean question about its pathology; what sickness of soul, we are moved to ask, would lead us to sacrifice so much for happiness so understood?[26] I do not wish to answer this question, so much as to register my agreement with the reason that prompts it.

We are therefore faced with a difficult problem. If neither of the two fundamental views of happiness stands on its own, how are we to synthesize them? I have claimed that we must begin with seeing a close connection between happiness and tranquillity, but I am also claiming that happiness is to be connected, in some sense, to activity, to the passions, and to assessment. How are restfulness and spiritual motion, or detachment and attachment, or inner peace and incompleteness, to be combined?

I have suggested that two senses of anxiety should be distinguished, the first an everyday anxiety about this or that thing (missing my plane, etc.), the second a general anxiety that things are out of kilter, formless, disintegrating. I also suggested a distinction between contentment and tranquillity, to be fleshed out later. Let us link up these distinctions as follows: the antidote to the first sort of anxiety is contentment. I make my plane, get the job I wanted, have a good meal; my anxiety about these things ends and I am satisfied for now. The antidote to the second sort of anxiety is tranquillity; at heart, I know who I am, how I fit into the whole scheme, and indeed that there is a whole scheme into which I fit.

Happiness provides a sense of reflective integration over time.[27] Happiness as tranquillity in this long-lasting, structural sense is compatible with anxiety and lack of contentment in the everyday sense. It is not reducible to what Hobbes calls "felicity," because it is not so much equanimity as it is equipoise, balance, and coherence in one's basic stance. By contrast, the anxious person in the second sense of the term is fundamentally disturbed, off-balance, never settled in the conviction that this is fundamentally the right way to spend one's life. The fittingness of one's basic stance is evident through reflection and, affectively, by the feeling that basically one would change nothing in one's life. One has lived and will live in this way; at that structural level, one is at rest, and tranquillity is correspondingly a sort of rest, of peacefulness, as I suggested at the start of this discussion.

One can and indeed must have all sorts of passions, attachments, commitments. These may well be turbulent at times; they certainly put one's happiness, in the sense of mood, at risk, for to some degree they put one's happiness in the hands of others. One's life may have moments of ecstasy or transcending bliss, and moments of anxiety in our first, ordinary sense of the term. Fortune will affect the course of things at this level. At the second-order level, however, one can be tranquil in the midst of first-order level perturbance, though not every perturbance. One can be peaceful but engaged. Take Epictetus' example of losing a wife or child. My child suddenly dies; on Epictetus' account, tranquillity seems to require no, or virtually no, emotional response (see also Plato *Republic* 603e ff.). On my account it would and ought naturally lead to tremendous grief, as is proportionate to the loss. I have not therefore lost my tranquillity; for I will still say that it was right and good that I had this child. I'm not sure I would take this to the absolute extreme, and say that a person enduring the tortures of a concentration camp could still be tranquil in my sense. But a person enduring the fate of a Socrates or Boethius might well be.[28]

Epictetus thought Socrates' tranquillity on his death bed explicable on the basis that Socrates was, in effect, a Stoic. While I see why one might make that argument, I do not believe that it is faithful either to what Socrates means when he says, in the *Phaedo*, that philosophy is a preparation for death, or to Socrates' praise of eros in other dialogues. My view of the relation between tranquillity and the tumult of ordinary life allows that Socrates would both experience great tranquillity in his lifelong commitment to philosophy, and also experience everything from pain caused by the shackles to sorrow at the prospect of death. Tranquillity does not require *apatheia*. My account allows us to understand both how philosophy might provide Socrates his tranquillity, and at the same time be the sort of painful dialectical struggle for truth depicted in Plato's dialogues and reenacted in so many philosophical conversations.

Epicurus is said to have claimed that the wise man could be happy (retain *ataraxia*) even on the rack.[29] My view does not make that extreme claim. There is no mathematically precise way to describe just how resistant tranquillity is to the misfortunes of life. I am claiming both that it is not absolutely resistant, and that the example of Socrates reminds us that tranquillity is within our grasp even in the context of great misfortune, if only we have developed a reflective stance to which our lives testify.

Happiness is, I have insisted, a feeling as well as a reflective stance. But it is not this or that feeling.[30] One might say, awkwardly, that it is a sort of second-order feeling. The feelings it attends will include those of satisfaction, joy, contentment, delight, perhaps bliss; and it will itself settle over them all as does the evening's light over the mountains. There will be shadows too—feelings of, say, frustration, incompleteness in this or that regard, regrets, and so forth. These are not incompatible with the judgment that as a whole one's life has been rightly oriented. The feeling of happiness signals a recognition that one is basically satisfied with who one is, and with reason; one does not want to be somebody else.

I have been sketching a way of reconciling two fundamental notions of happiness. I have attempted, among other things, to articulate that paradoxical mix of activity and passivity, of self-directedness and of feeling as though one is being carried by events in the direction one would wish for, that characterizes the experience of happiness. But first it is important to reflect on the distinction between happiness and contentment.

II. HAPPINESS AND CONTENTMENT

> For who is content is happy. But as soon as any new uneasiness comes in, this Happiness is disturb'd, and we are set afresh on work in the pursuit of Happiness.
> —John Locke[31]

Tranquillity and contentment resemble one another, especially when one focuses on the feelings involved. The contented person has what she wants, and enough of the things one ordinarily desires, and is satisfied with that.[32] But one could be content on and off, as when we speak of being content while on vacation, that is, until we submerge again in "the real world," as we mistakenly call it; and contentment can disappear rather quickly, as when one is content until one has to go to the dentist for a root canal. Then, as Locke says in the passage quoted immediately above, a "new uneasiness" has set in. I could be content with my job interview in the sense that it went well, but be very unhappy generally, including with the whole path of life on which this job interview, indeed this job, are steps. One can be contented, even contented repeatedly, without being happy.

And even if one possessed what Hobbes calls "felicity," there is a more important way in which it is distinguished from happiness as I have characterized it; and that is the tendency of contentment to reduce itself to a state of mind severed from an appraisal of the truth of the matter. Contentment and unreflectiveness are natural allies. At the extreme, the content are, so to speak, tranquillized. I have in mind the figure of the contented slave, or the contented sinner; someone resigned to the limitations of life, someone for whom the link between the subjective feeling and an assessment of the worthiness of his life is broken.[33] It is for this reason that Nietzsche heaps such scorn on happiness understood as contentment, and Heidegger portrays daily existence as "inauthentic" and as mired unreflectively in the "everyday."[34] Contentment is the road to mediocrity. It is often compared to the life of the beasts, not without reason; my dog, for example, can certainly be happy in the sense of content. When you doze after a fine meal, you are not happy, however peaceful you may be. You are semiconscious, and contented.

One could reply that we sometimes use the word "contentment" to refer precisely to the sort of reflective tranquillity I have sketched above, and "happiness" in reference to, say, one's dog. I grant the objection, but it is merely a verbal point. We also use the words in the sense I am now isolating, and we recognize the distinction between the phenomena in question.

The confusion between happiness and contentment is, nevertheless, widespread. The often belated recognition that the two are distinct is perhaps not as widespread, but it is the stuff of which the wisdom of the elders is made. The confusion is so systematic that it has been used quite persuasively by Adam Smith to explain why it is that people strive so mightily for goods that will not, in fact, bring them happiness. Taking his cue from Hobbes, Smith sees us as naturally bent on what he calls "bettering our condition." We better our condition by accumulating the "goods of fortune"—external goods, as well as wealth, reputation, and power. We do so not in order to satisfy our bodily desires, Smith argues, but in order to find ourselves the objects of approbation; for therein, we imagine, lies happiness (TMS 1.3.2.1). Smith refers to this as a "prejudice" of the imagination, and as a "deception." Smith remarks that a man who imagines himself in the condition of the rich "thinks if he had attained all these [good things], he would sit still contentedly, and be quiet, enjoying himself in the thought of the happiness and tranquillity of his situation. He is enchanted with the distant idea of this felicity" (TMS 4.1.8, p. 181).

And to attain that superior station, he labors day and night, achieving moments of contentment, but always anxious to progress a bit further, to earn that much more admiration from society. At what point does he see that he has sacrificed "a real tranquillity that is at all times in his power"? It is in old age, once he has attained wealth and power, as he lies "in the last dregs of life, his body wasted with toil and diseases, his mind galled and ruffled by the memory of a thousand injuries and disappointments which he imagines he has met with from the injustice of his enemies, or from the perfidy and ingratitude of his friends, that he begins at last to find that wealth and greatness are mere trinkets of frivolous utility, no more adapted for procuring ease of body or tranquillity of mind than the tweezer-cases of the lover of toys" (TMS 4.1.8, p. 181). Then he sees the difference between contentment and real tranquillity.

In Smith's vignette, the unhappy social climber gains self-knowledge in recognizing that happiness is tranquillity. With that recognition, he regrets how he spent his life. He knows, somewhere in his soul, that he does not deserve to be happy, and so is not happy. He is not what he says he is. A sense of guilt, and an anxiety about being found out, bubble underneath the surface of his life. This is not an uncommon experience; it buttresses the case I am making for a distinction between happiness and contentment. In this way I grant Kant's distinction between happiness and the worthiness to be happy; except that the former I view as contentment, and the latter as happiness.[35]

Smith's compelling picture of what others would call the life of the bourgeois shows that, on an individual level, that life is vulnerable. This sort of "happiness" is vulnerable, for example, to political or social upheavals.[36] And there is never enough of "the good things" to constitute happiness. The pursuit of happiness, so understood, can never rest. The notion of happiness I have sketched above, by contrast, allows for the desired stability and security.

I have argued, however, that there are objective criteria for happiness. Let me offer four rather extreme examples by way of illustrating this point. First: suppose that a drug were invented and were dripped into one's veins, painlessly and continuously.[37] Let us pretend that the technical name of this drug is "Ataraxy." Suppose further that Ataraxy made one unaware that one was taking it. As a result one would experience contentment over the long haul, even though one's life alternated between prolonged periods as a couch potato watching soap operas, and indulgence in violent "drive-by" murders. We would want to deny that such a person is happy, however complete the feeling of tranquillity may be. For the person on Ataraxy to say of himself that he is happy (as always, in our long-range sense) is at a minimum to say that his tranquillity reflects his life's activities in a satisfying way. This in turn assumes that the person is fully aware of what those activities are. If Ataraxy prevents this awareness, then he is not happy. If Ataraxy allows this awareness, then he might be happy, but only if he has made no mistake about these activities and their capacity to satisfy. He must believe that it is "all right" to do what he does; but if he is wrong in this belief then he is not happy. Happiness is linked to beliefs about the world, and these can be true or false.

Suppose, to take another example, someone thinks herself very happy because she thinks she has discovered that Elvis lives. Impartial spectators investigate, and find that a very clever impostor has tricked her. She experienced contentment, even delight, in her belief. But since her belief was false, was she truly happy? I do not think so; for her life is not such as she would wish it to be on reflection, in the light of an accurate assessment of the situation. Or if she is truly happy, then why would she not be truly happy when on Ataraxy?

A third example: Say a homeless man woke up one day in his habitual spot, a heating vent on the sidewalk, fantasizing that he is rich. Suppose the fantasy takes hold; he believes himself to be Mr. Onassis at his winter château in Gstaad. The homeless man is very happy. Or is he? He is living in a dream world and is delighted with life, but surely he is not happy. It is not true that ignorance is bliss; he is vulnerable in his ignorance (for example, to hunger). This is not a formula for long-term tranquillity, for the sense of happiness under investigation here. It may be counted as a formula for short-term contentment at best.

Further, "happiness" by self-deluded fantasy seems truncated. As the man lies on the heating vent, he pictures the adoration bestowed on the wealthy and powerful and imagines himself its object; but he does not know their lives, their conversations, their failures, their triumphs. The image he conjures up in his dream life is a cartoon, and so at best a truncated partaking, and does not measure up to its own object.

Consider a fourth example. Suppose a woman habitually drinks too much and then regrets it the next morning. Suppose she goes on like that for years. While high, she is content; in the cold light of sobriety, as she contemplates her blood-shot eyes and pudgy face in the morning's mirror, she realizes that she is terribly unhappy, and that the contentment she finds in the bottle is a flight from the underlying deficiency of her life. This sort of experience is common, and reveals several important truths, one of which is that one cannot be happy if one harbors a well-grounded standing dissatisfaction with oneself, with how one really is.[38] And that suggests that to be happy one must have the sort of desires a reflective person would want. This helps explain why we place such a premium on long-term happiness; we see that such happiness is connected to a well-ordered life, one that is worth having.

Examples such as these suggest that while happiness is inseparable from a state of mind, it is distinguished from contentment because it is also inseparable from a reflective arrangement of one's life, and more deeply because any such arrangement of one's life must be evaluatively linked to a notion of what sort of life is worth living. Happiness is not to be understood simply as a state of mind.

The erroneous notions of happiness implied in the above examples suffer from three defects. First, that "happiness" is unstable. Because it is unstable, it is vulnerable. What one does not know *can* hurt one. Consider an example from *Othello*. Thinking Desdemona unfaithful, Othello cries: "I had been happy, if the general camp, / Pioneers and all, had tasted her sweet body, / So I had nothing known. O, now for ever / Farewell the tranquil mind! farewell content!" (Shakespeare *Othello* 3.3.1.347–50). Othello is unhappy in a false belief; he says he would rather be ignorant and happy, but in fact the dramatic irony of the scene shows us the opposite. He would in fact be happy if he had known the truth, as the tragic ending of the play underlines. This is not simply because the truth is what he wants to hear. I would hold that he would likely have been happier even if Desdemona had been unfaithful.

Happiness based on self-delusion is also susceptible to the power of the question, as when the alcoholic is made to confront head-on the question "Why are you drinking?" I do not mean that a confrontation with the question will of itself change behavior; I mean that conceits about the "happiness" supposedly provided by the alcohol are vulnerable to severe deflation. They do not stand up to (self-) questioning. I have said, however, that I am investigating "happiness" in the long-range sense, one that requires a stability of self.

136218

Second, even if the deluded state of mind were stable in the sense of temporally long-lasting, we cannot say of it that it is "happiness" without entering into an evaluative reflection about the sorts of things or activities that provide this happiness. But this is what is missing from that state of mind.

Third, if one's experience is that of a fantasy rather than of the real thing, whatever "happiness" one derives is not a product of one's being, or doing, the real thing. If when high on booze an alcoholic imagines herself happy because beloved by a family to which she is devoted, whereas in fact her family is in tatters precisely because of her drinking; is her "happiness" of the same quality or depth as that which stems from really being loved by a family to which one really is devoted? I am suggesting that we are faithful to experience in distinguishing similarly between the "happiness" a drunkard imagines and the happiness she would possess if it were a product of reality and not fantasy.

I have been arguing that happiness is linked to a reflective affirmation of one's life. Contentment may be thought of as the satisfaction of desire(s); happiness, as the justified satisfaction that one is desiring the right things in the right way. There is therefore a connection between happiness and our conception of happiness; one needs a right understanding of it in order to have it. Since a conception of happiness must be acquired with effort, and since patterning one's life on that conception also takes effort, it follows from my account that happiness cannot simply happen to a person. Happiness requires effort. This parallels Aristotle's account of the connection between happiness and both virtues and *phronesis*. Virtues and *phronesis* do not come, in their full sense, automatically; they require sustained exertion and exercise.

III. PHILOSOPHY AND HAPPINESS

They do not understand how that which differs with itself
is in agreement: harmony consists of opposing tension, like
that of the bow and the lyre.
                                        —Heraclitus[39]

Let us say that I am tranquil in the sense described thus far. For good reasons I am satisfied with my basic stance; I am committed to the right sorts of things, in the right way, and I act accordingly. I have no significant standing dissatisfactions with myself; I have the sort of wants I would wish to have on reflection; I am reasonably well ordered; basically I am complete. Let us also say, so as to simplify, that I am neither in agony nor in despair in a day-to-day sense. Tranquillity requires assessment, evaluation of my stance; otherwise it would be difficult to distinguish between contentment and tranquillity. The question "am I happy?" develops, on my account, into the question "am I, on the whole, the sort of person I ought to be?" The assessment required by the latter question is a philosophical one. From Socrates on down through the tradition, the questions "who am I?" and "what sort of person ought I be?" are fundamental to the philosophical enterprise. The term *philosophical*, however, is said in many ways, two of which interest me here. One sense of the term is used by the Stoics especially. There it denotes something like dialogue that leads not to the investigation of epistemological or metaphysical theses, but to clarification of principles that will permit a tranquil life. That is, "philosophy" is something like the art of living; its orientation is practical rather than theoretical. Insofar as Epictetus' *Discourses* resist a turn towards speculative theory, and are intended simply to explain and defend a few basic principles as well as what is required to live in accordance with them, these dialogues are remarkably unSocratic, especially if Plato's portrait of Socrates is taken as the standard.[40] There is no upward, erotic ascent in Epictetus' dialectic; nothing of the Socratic passion for knowledge or sense of *aporia*.

Correspondingly, as in so many "philosophies of life," there is a great deal that philosophy, in a more Socratic/Platonic sense, would find question-begging. *Philosophy* in this second sense—the sense I shall use—would surely attack the connection between happiness, tranquillity, and control. But my task here is to argue that the sort of bothersome questions Plato's Socrates pursues are necessarily connected with the rational assessment of self I have made necessary to happiness.[41] I do not mean that the answers one ends up with are those of Socrates; I mean that the kind of dialogical reflection in which one engages is like that of Socrates. It is full of *aporiai*, yielding of further questions, never straightforwardly self-justifying, always lacking and incomplete.

Philosophy so understood is a passionate activity, and usually a painful dialectical labor as well. But that in itself does not establish any tension between it and happiness as I have described it, since I have argued that meta-level tranquillity and object-level perturbation are compatible. One need not agree with Aristotle that "the pleasures of gaining knowledge involve no pain" (*Nicomachean Ethics* 10.3.1173b16–17), or that the life of contemplation and philosophy contains pleasures of wondrous purity (*Nicomachean Ethics* 10.6.1177a 25–27), in order to maintain the link between tranquillity and philosophy. Aristotle's picture in the *Ethics* of the theoretical life is idealized and abstracts from philosophizing as it is in actuality.

The perpetual incompleteness and self-overcoming of this particular sort of activity, however, does suggest an underlying incompatibility with happiness. The philosopher will, on the one hand, naturally ascend from questions about human phenomena to second-order questions about whether this or that is the right stance to take towards the world, eventually settling on the philosophical stance, precisely as Socrates does over and over again in Plato's dialogues. When Socrates declares that the "unexamined life is not worth living for a human being" (Plato *Apology* 38a5–6) he is declaring his allegiance to that stance. And yet, on the other hand, one of the con- sistent themes in the Platonic dialogues concerns the nature and defensibility of the philosophical life. But this is just to say that the stability of a general stance towards the world, that framework which permitted tranquillity in the midst of turbulence, is undermined and itself thrown into motion. One becomes just as Socrates describes eros in the *Symposium*; in-between, lacking, desiring to overcome, perpetually in motion between poles of ignorance and wisdom, but also with resourcefulness. This is why Socrates never says that philosophizing is happiness or a happy activity (*Phr.* 256a7–b3 notwithstanding), though Crito thinks Socrates always of happy temperament and remarks on his amazing calmness as he awaits exe- cution. In Plato's portrayal, only on the day of his death does Socrates smile.

Wisdom, by contrast, is portrayed by Socrates as supreme happiness (*Phr.* 247d; *Symposium* 212a; *Republic* 516c). For the wise, motion and rest are harmonized; this is captured rather beautifully by the image of the circular rotation of νοῦς, i.e., of the activity of mind that is contemplation by the wise (*Phr.* 247b6–e6). Happiness is this activity of simultaneous rest and repose. But, Socrates also tells us, wisdom is impossible in this life. Consequently, it would seem that happiness is impossible in this life. Thus happiness is impossible without philosophy and impossible with it.

Or is it? Consider the following. Both the practice of philosophizing and reflections about finitude and our desire to overcome it leave us with this picture: human beings are perpetually incomplete, and when they reflect dialectically about that incompleteness, they are engaged in philosophy. From this bird's-eye perspective, one sees that the stance represented by the philosophical life is superior relative to its competitors; one sees that the philosophical life is not absolutely defensible so much as it is relatively defensible against all comers to date. One sees that by means of it, false alternatives have been isolated; the features of the real alternatives have been discerned and brought into question. A metaphysics takes shape correspondingly; it provides a way of contextualizing human life in an ordered cosmos. This metaphysics will itself be held open to question, as is only appropriate given that we are not wise but are lovers of wisdom. It will amount to what Socrates calls "human wisdom" (*Apology* 20d8). The philosopher will ask whether he has cooked up this metaphysics in a desperate attempt to make himself happy (as Socrates himself wonders at *Phil.* 28c), or whether it provides the best explanation of the phenomena. Has the philosopher shown only that any competing view that offers a logos can be out-argued? I would argue that in its openness to question, even our most basic framework confirms the authority of the philosophical life, for that life consists precisely in posing questions and seeking answers, always with an awareness of the possibility that one's answers are open to further reasonable questions. Does this self-confirmation amount to genuine openness, or to closure? Is it circular in a good or bad sense? The Socratic philosopher will recognize these questions as his or her own.

I am merely sketching the sort of answer I would give to the problem I raised about my own view of happiness.[42] I am suggesting that reflection on philosophy itself provides a sort of ledge on which one can sit, not with complete safety, but still with stability. That place is integrated with a commitment to philosophy, as well as the day-to-day activity of philosophizing about this or that. Questioning the niche we have attained philosophically confirms it performatively, since it is an instance of the very activity that we call philosophy. This metaphysical position may be far from the summit, but on the other hand it is far enough up so as to afford perspective and the long view. To that extent, it is the basis for whatever tranquillity nature has afforded us, and it is compatible with turbulence at both the first- and second-order levels of reflection. Differently put, that stance which is the philosophical life may be espoused in a *measured* way; in a manner that is proportionate to our self-knowledge. In its measuredness, it is tranquil.

Let me close with a reformulation of the connection between philosophy and tranquillity I have been sketching. Happiness, understood as tranquillity, might metaphorically be understood as motion in a circle that is at rest. That circle or framework or stance provides the stability within which activity, passion, striving, philosophizing, are oriented. Since Socratic philosophers also feel compelled to question philosophy itself, that is, their own circle or framework or stance, they seem to undermine the basis for their own tranquillity. That process of self-undermining, however, is itself an instance of philosophizing, and therefore is confirming of philosophy as indispensable to reflective self-knowledge. The recognition that this is so as well as the recognition that even this thesis cannot be held dogmatically, are themselves the circle or framework or stance that—aporetically—form the basis for tranquillity. No tranquillity of this sort can perfectly combine rest and motion. We will never be those Platonic souls who, perfected, rest while circling and feasting on the divine. They are carried around in a comprehensive vision of truth, and need only sit still and let the mind nourish itself. So as to become like them, we must originate our own motion, and rest tranquil in the recognition that our circle is philosophical.[43]

NOTES

1. Adam Smith, *The Theory of Moral Sentiments*, ed. A. L. Macfie and D. D. Raphael (Indianapolis: Liberty Classics, 1982), 3.5.7, p. 166. (Hereafter abbreviated TMS.)

2. For an excellent treatment of Hegel on happiness, see A. W. Wood, *Hegel's Ethical Thought* (Cambridge: Cambridge University Press, 1991), chap. 3.

3. I refer to Sidgwick, *The Methods of Ethics* reprint ed. (Indianapolis: Hackett, 1981), bk. 2, chaps. 5, 6, *et passim*.

4. Bertrand Russell, *The Conquest of Happiness* (New York: H. Liveright, 1930).

5. See J. Annas, *The Morality of Happiness* (Oxford: Oxford University Press, 1993); E. Telfer, *Happiness* (New York: St. Martin's Press, 1980); S. Strasser, "The Experience of Happiness: A Phenomenological Typology,"

in *Readings in Existential Phenomenology*, ed. N. Lawrence and D. O'Connor (Englewood Cliffs, N.J.: Prentice-Hall, 1967), pp. 286–302. For a review and bibliography of other literature see D. Den Uyl and T. R. Machan, "Recent Work on the Concept of Happiness," *American Philosophical Quarterly* 20 (1983): 115–34.

    6. Kant provides one explanation in Immanuel Kant, *Fundamental Principles of the Metaphysics of Ethics*, trans. T. K. Abbott (Indianapolis: Hackett, 1949), pp. 35–36. See also Immanuel Kant, *Critique of Practical Reason*, trans. L. W. Beck, 3rd ed. (New York: Macmillan, 1993), pp. 20, 25. My argument about happiness is incompatible with that presented by Kant in the text just cited.

    7. Aristotle grants that people have different things in mind when they speak of happiness, but sees them as competing specifications of the same generally shared understanding of happiness as "the good life" (τὸ εὖ ζῆν) or "doing well" (τὸ εὖ πράττειν). That happiness so understood is that good at which politics aims is, he also says, the opinion of nearly everyone (*Nicomachean Ethics* 1.4.1095a14–21). These assertions are facilitated to some extent by the word he is using for "happiness" (*eudaimonia*), and they pave the way for his understanding of "doing well" as "activity of soul in accordance with excellence." They are thus crucial to the progress of his argument; both may, however, be disputed. For example, Kant did reject them.

    8. This "empirical question" is, I admit, notoriously difficult to substantiate. For an attempt at an empirical determination of what people say about their own happiness, see T. Scitovsky, *The Joyless Economy: The Psychology of Human Satisfaction*, rev. ed. (New York: Oxford University Press, 1992), esp. chap. 7 ("Income and Happiness"). Perhaps it is instructive to listen to the testimony of those who have succeeded in accumulating wealth: Ross Perot declared in his Commencement address at Boston University on May 22, 1994, that he knows personally almost all of the very rich people in the world and that virtually none of them is happy.

    9. Annas remarks: "The development of the debate about virtue and happiness from Aristotle through the Stoics to Antiochus rests on this point of method: how much of the content of our initial intuitions about happiness is it important to retain?" The debate concerned in part the "choice of candidate for giving us the content of happiness—pleasure, tranquillity, virtue and so on" (Annas, *The Morality of Happiness*, p. 233).

    10. Aristotle *Nicomachean Ethics* 1.7.1098a18–20 (trans. M. Ostwald, pp. 17–18). Unless otherwise noted, all reference to the *Nicomachean Ethics* advert to this translation.

    11. Smith, TMS 3.3.30, p. 149.

    12. Compare Rousseau's remarks about happiness in the fifth Promenade (Jean-Jacques Rousseau, *The Reveries of the Solitary Walker*,

trans. C. Butterworth [New York: New York University Press, 1979], pp. 68–69).

13. In this paragraph I draw upon L. Edmunds, *Cleon, Knights, and Aristophanes' Politics* (Lanham, Va.: University Press of America, 1987), chap. 2.

14. Epictetus *Discourses* 4.4.34–38, 6.34; 4.7.27–33; *Encheiridion* 29.7.

15. Thomas Hobbes, *Leviathan*, ed. C. B. MacPherson (Baltimore: Penguin Books, 1972), pp. 129–30.

16. Ibid., pp. 160–61. For a similar contrast between "uneasiness" and "happiness" see John Locke *Essay* 2.21.42–46.

17. My distinction between the two kinds of anxiety parallels (though it may not be the same as) Heidegger's distinction between fear and *angst* in *Being and Time* 1.6 sec. 40. Heidegger there says that in the latter one feels "uncanny" (or "unfamiliar," "not at home"; *unheimlich*), which would naturally seem to be an anxious feeling. By 2.3, however, Heidegger speaks briefly of this *angst* as bringing "joy" along with it.

18. This point is also made by Rémi Brague in *Aristote et la question du monde* (Paris: Presses Universitaires de France, 1988), p. 477: "He [Aristotle] aims above all to establish the superiority of the contemplative life. In doing so, he thematizes only the *content* of happiness. The act of being happy *qua* act, in its realization, remains implicit. Aristotle has not described the experience of happiness. Yet he knows perfectly well that the act contains an internal actuality, as one might put it" (my translation).

19. He also notes at *Nicomachean Ethics* 2.3.1104b24–25 that some thinkers say that the virtues are states of "ἀπαθείας" and "ἠρεμίας," i.e., of lack of passion and rest or quietness. He rejects that view on the grounds that it omits to add "in the right manner" and "at the right time"; but he does not reject the notion completely.

20. Aristotle asks, "Why should we not call happy the man who exercises his abilities according to the highest standards of virtue and excellence in a context which affords him sufficient resources and not merely for a brief moment but throughout his life?" (*Nicomachean Ethics* 1.10.110a14–16 [trans. J. Lear in *Aristotle: The Desire to Understand* (Cambridge: Cambridge University Press, 1988), p. 155. A person objecting along the lines I have indicated might respond: "Why should we?"

21. See Aristotle *Nicomachean Ethics* 10.4.1175a13–15: "Life is an activity (ἐνέργεια), and each man actively exercises (ἐνεργεῖ) his favorite faculties upon the objects he loves most. A man who is musical, for example, exercises his hearing upon tunes, an intellectual (Φιλομαθὴς) his thinking upon the subjects of his study (τὰ θεωρήματα), and so forth."

22. Epictetus *Encheiridion* 11.

23. Ibid., 26.

24. Epictetus *Discourses* 4.4.36–37.

25. Ibid., 4.4.33. (I have slightly emended the translation.)

26. See, for example, Nietzsche, *Beyond Good and Evil* 1.9.

27. For some helpful reflections on the temporal dimension of this integration, see Brague, *Aristote*, pp. 479–81.

28. For a moving testimony to the power of Epictetus' philosophy to save one's integrity and happiness in a situation that is close to that of a concentration camp, see J. B. Stockdale, "Courage under Fire: Testing Epictetus' Doctrines in a Laboratory of Human Behavior" (Stanford: Hoover Institution Essays, Stanford University, 1993). The "laboratory" is a North Vietnamese prison camp, in which Admiral Stockdale spent eight years, and in which he was repeatedly tortured.

29. See Diogenes Laertius *Lives* 10.118.

30. Here I am in agreement with R. Barrow, *Happiness and Schooling* (New York: St. Martin's Press, 1980), pp. 66–67.

31. John Locke, *An Essay Concerning Human Understanding*, ed. P. H. Nidditch (Oxford: Clarendon, 1990), 2.21.59 (p. 273).

32. For a useful description of "contentment," see Strasser, "The Experience of Happiness," pp. 286–88. On p. 287 Strasser remarks: "The contented person has all that he wants, because he wants nothing that he cannot have; and thus he succeeds also in being happy."

33. One could adduce the example of the happy tyrant (if there is such a thing) to the same effect. This is a notion discussed by Socrates and Polus in the *Gorgias* 469a ff., and in Xenophon's *Hiero*.

34. I have in mind Friedrich Nietzsche, *Thus Spoke Zarathustra*, Part III, "On Virtue that Makes Small"; and Heidegger *Being and Time* 1.4–5 *et passim*. By contrast, consider the distinction between happiness and contentment in Rousseau's ninth Promenade: "Happiness is a permanent condition which does not seem to be made for man here below. Everything on earth is in constant flux, which permits nothing to take on a constant form. Everything around us changes. . . . Let us take advantage of mental contentment when it comes. . . . I have seldom seen happy men, perhaps not at all. But I have often seen contented hearts; and of all the objects which have struck me, that is the one which has made me most content" (Rousseau, *Reveries of the Solitary Walker*, p. 122).

35. For Kant's distinction see the *Critique of Practical Reason*, p. 136: "morals is not really the doctrine of how to make ourselves happy but of how we are to be *worthy* of happiness."

36. As Strasser nicely puts it: the contented person "can feel at peace only so long as he knows his position is secure. This characteristic also points up the fragility of the happiness of contentment. It is not able to flourish on volcanic soil, in epochs which are shaken by spiritual fever and crises" ("The

Experience of Happiness"), p. 288. The person who seeks "happiness" *qua* contentment is naturally and literally "conservative," precisely as Smith indicates in the TMS.

37. A thought experiment of this sort is elaborated by Robert Nozick in the chapter on happiness in *The Examined Life* (New York: Simon and Schuster, 1989), pp. 104–5. Recent discussion about the drug "Prozac" touches on the issues I am about to raise by means of the fictitious drug "Ataraxy."

38. My formulation is close to but less subjective than that of R. Montague in his "Happiness," *Proceedings of the Aristotelian Society* N.S. 67 (1967), p. 87: "One logically necessary condition of happiness seems then to be that the happy person should have no standing dissatisfactions which are serious from his point of view."

39. Diels, *Ancilla to the Pre-Socratic Philosophers*, trans. Kathleen Freeman (Cambridge: Harvard University Press, 1983), p. 28.

40. For example, see the discussion in Heraclitus *Discourses* 4.4.14–18, on reading philosophy books, and on what philosophy has to teach us; 2.12. on "the art of argumentation [dialectic]"; and the wonderful dialogue at 1.29.22–29.35, about the practical utility of a philosophy course.

41. There is an alternative way of understanding the sought-for assessment, however, viz., one that unfolds within the context of religious faith. Given the complexities involved in meeting the counterexample provided by revealed religion especially, I must postpone the response for another occasion. The (Socratic) approach I would take would, of course, include questioning the basic principles held in faith by the reflective religious person.

42. For a full discussion of philosophy so understood I refer the reader to my "Plato's Metaphilosophy: Why Plato Wrote Dialogues," in *Platonic Writings, Platonic Readings*, ed. Charles Griswold (New York: Routledge, Chapman, and Hall, 1988), pp. 143–67.

43. I am indebted to Rémi Brague, Ronna Burger, Bob Cohen, Ed Delattre, Doug Den Uyl, Steven Griswold, Drew Hyland, Knud Haakonssen, Erazim Kohak, Mitch Miller, Christopher Ricks, David Roochnik, Lee Rouner, Jim Schmidt, Roger Scruton, Roger Shattuck, and Fred Tauber, for their comments on earlier drafts of this paper. This essay was presented on Feb. 23, 1994, as part of Boston University's Institute for Philosophy and Religion series "In Pursuit of Happiness." Subsequent drafts were presented at the annual meetings of the American Philosophical Association (December 1994) and at Vassar College (January 1995).

Happiness in Motion: Desire and Delight

MARGARET R. MILES

Delight orders the soul; where the soul's delight is, there
is its treasure.

—De musica 6.11.29

PLATO, ARISTOTLE, PLOTINUS, AND AUGUSTINE had ideas of human
happiness that have influenced Western philosophy and theology
to our own time, ideas that inform our concepts of happiness and
the human good. I will first describe Plato's, Aristotle's, and Plotinus'
distinctive proposals about the nature of human happiness and how
it is to be achieved. I will then examine Augustine's revisions of the
classical ideas he inherited. Throughout I will highlight one of the
issues most central to discussions of happiness, namely the role
of the body and sensuous life in happiness. Can "real" happiness be
achieved and maintained, as some have suggested, only by excluding
the vulnerability necessarily entailed in enjoyment of sense, sexuality,
and relationship? Or are these familiar joys so integral that they must
be a part of any happy life? Anyone asked to reflect on happiness can
be expected to have a rather personal interest in the topic. And I do.
And so it would be an evasion of the assignment if I did not en-
deavor to construct for you my own idea of happiness and to analyze
its constituent supports. The last part of my essay will do this, not
because I suppose that I can think about the issue more clearly and
competently than the giants of the past, but because, although I
am heavily indebted to their thought, I am differently positioned in
human history. For myriad reasons, my proposal of what constitutes
happiness will necessarily be somewhat different from theirs, even
though owing a great deal to their proposals.

I

For the Greeks, the happy, deeply satisfying life is the good life. Agreeing on that, they diverged in identifying its components, its requirements, and its characteristic activity. Recently Martha Nussbaum's intriguing book, *The Fragility of Goodness*, has discussed Greek philosophers' "central preoccupation" with the human good. Underlying and motivating this preoccupation, she writes, was "a raw sense of the passivity of human beings and their humanity in a world of nature, [together with] a response of both horror and anger at that passivity."[1] Human life needs redemption from this vulnerability to luck (*tyche*) or fate, to "what just *happens* to a person, as opposed to what [a person] does or makes." In the face of terrifying vulnerability, Nussbaum writes, Greek thinkers held the belief that reason's activity could make one safe, and thereby save the person "from living at the mercy of luck."[2]

For example, Plato's resolution of the Greek problem was to posit the possibility of a "self-sufficient and purely rational" human life.[3] The classical example of such a life of developed and concentrated rationality was that a person ought to be perfectly happy while being roasted alive in that ancient instrument of the cruelest torture, the bull of Phalaris. In the person with fully developed rationality, no amount of pain, loss, or terror could damage one's equanimity or loosen one's grip on a rational process that remained untouched by the inevitable incursions of fate. In short, Plato's solution to the problem of human vulnerability was transcendence based on a thoroughgoing recognition and acceptance of the limitations of physical life in the world of nature, and on self-identification with immortal Reason.

Thus far, however, we have gotten no further than our received picture of Plato's "disdain for the body." There is, however, more complexity to Plato's thought than this. He was not unaware that identification with rationality did rather neglect some of what Nussbaum calls our most "familiar and prized activities and allegiances," those organized by "our bodily and sensuous nature, our passions, our sexuality." And, of course, all of these are "powerful links to the world of risk [instability] and mutability."[4] How is that enormous range of things that are both necessary and pleasurable—from nourishment to sexuality—to be distributed in relation to the human good? As Nussbaum puts it, "We would like to find a way to retain our identity as desiring and moving beings, and yet to make ourselves self-sufficient."[5] Plato's answer to this dilemma, described most point-edly in the *Symposium*, is not a concept or an ideal but a method. It is worth listening again to his account of the redemption of human life from contingency and vulnerability:

> [The one] who would proceed aright . . . should begin in youth to visit beautiful forms: and first, if he be guided by his instructor aright, to love one such form only . . . and soon he will of himself perceive that the beauty of one form is akin to the beauty of an-other; and then, if beauty of form in general is his pursuit, how foolish would he be not to recognize that the beauty in every form is one and the same! And when he perceives this he will abate his violent love of the one . . . and will become a lover of all beautiful forms: in the next stage he will perceive that the beauty of the mind is more honorable than the beauty of the outward form. [He will then move on] to contemplate the beauty of institutions and laws and to understand that the beauty of them all is of one family; . . . and after laws and institutions he will go on to sciences, that he may see their beauty. . . .[6]

"Ascending under the influence of love," *collecting*, not discarding, particulars from the world of the senses, the student will come at last to a vision of "beauty absolute, separate, simple and everlasting." The method outlined here is to "begin from the beauties of earth and mount upwards . . . until [the lover of beauty] arrives at the notion of absolute beauty and at last knows what the essence of beauty is."[7] "True beauty," Plato says, is "not clogged with the pollutions of mortality and all the colors and illusions of human life." Thus, moved by the energy of enthralled love from "one beautiful body," to beautiful forms, beau-tiful practices, and beautiful ideas, one gradually isolates the element common to all of these disparate entities: the reality of beauty. Modern people would call this a process of abstraction, a process by which par-ticularity, "color," and the perennial ambiguities of human experience vanish in—or are caught up in—"beauty absolute, separate, and ever-lasting." Beauty "pure and unalloyed" is a vision of beauty accessible only to the trained eye, the eye trained by disciplined recognition of myriad beauties.[8] The most careful exposition of Plato's thought must reflect, rather than resolve, the irreducible ambiguity of his attitude toward "the silken weavings of our afternoons."[9]

Plato has made two proposals in this passage about how to enjoy sensual pleasures without placing oneself in a slavish and vulnerable position. First, what one loves in "one beautiful body" is not its uniqueness but its beauty, which is, after all, a repeatable and replaceable entity, a quality, in fact, shared by all beautiful bodies. If the "one beautiful body" is lost, it can be replaced by another. Secondly, and even more dramatically, one *kind* of beauty is *the same as* another: contemplation of beautiful bodies, or beautiful ideas, or beautiful ways of life gives roughly the same pleasure. What one irreducibly *has*, in the generosity of the universe, is what Plato calls a "sea of beauty." One can, then—and must—relax one's intransigent requirement that gratification must come from the one person one loves, and adjust one's love to beauty itself, in whatever form, wherever it is found. And it is found everywhere, Plato says; it is continuously adjacent to senses and intellect. Having recognized beauty in its collected and concentrated form, it pops into the eye everywhere.

This is the happy life. Plato, like Aristotle after him, will not scruple to call the possessor of such a life "divine" because she is not at the mercy of "whatever happens" but has become adept at focusing the vision of beauty-which-*is*-happiness. Thus the happy life is invulnerable, relying not at all on circumstances. The happy life is also individual. This is necessary to its invulnerability. It needs neither other people, nor society; indeed, it may be practiced in a more concentrated and focused way in isolation, though it is pleasant to confer with others occasionally; it is pleasant to whet one's mental powers by detecting and exposing their clumsy misunderstandings. It helps to have friends like those of Socrates, if one can find them—gentle people who do not interrupt one's train of thought with rude rebuttals. Rather they sit—or stroll—about saying, "Quite right, Socrates," to everything one says. Facetiousness aside, for Plato, friends are useful in the philosophic life; friends egg one another on in virtue and vision.

Aristotle's proposal for the happy life revised Plato's ideal of self-sufficiency and invulnerability. Aristotle acknowledged the possibility that determined and practiced self-identification with rationality might not be enough to make human life good, and therefore happy. He admitted that certain calamities—debilitating illness, severe financial reverses, or the loss of those most dear—can, and regularly do, substantially alter a person, damaging personality and morality. For

Aristotle, the good life is irreducibly and necessarily vulnerable, dependent on luck, external goods, health, and unimpeded voluntary action. In fact, the happier a person is, and the more she possesses, the more at risk she is of losing the resources and circumstances that have contributed to her happiness. For this reason Aristotle cautioned: "Call no one happy until he is dead." The possibility of dramatic reversals of fortune lasts as long as a human life. Yet Aristotle did not advise renunciation of those goods and pleasures that make one most vulnerable to loss—love of other human beings, material possessions, the pleasures of the senses. Rather, in Nussbaum's words:

> the goal of the Aristotelian is not so much happiness in the sense of contentment as it is fullness of life and richness of value; it is not a solution to omit a value for happiness's sake, to reduce your demands on the world in order to get pleasing answers from the world. The Aristotelian will simply take on the world and see what can be done with it.[10]

Aristotle begins his discussion of happiness in Book Ten of the *Nicomachean Ethics* by stipulating that happiness must be an activity rather than a state. But what kind of an activity? One that is desirable for its own sake and, preferably, one that needs few external circumstances or resources. Obviously, pleasant amusements do not qualify. They "need" too much: health, a relaxed mind, and the price of the ticket, to name only a few. Virtuous actions, then? Yes, but not the sort of virtuous actions that depend on the existence of a preexisting need and a recipient. Rather, Aristotle says, the most virtuous activities are those that flow directly and spontaneously from one's nature. It is not a long step from here to his agreement with Plato that since reason is the "best part" of human beings, virtue, and with it happiness, will lie in the exercise, the *activity*, of *this* part. Contemplation is this activity, and, perhaps predictably, since a philosopher is describing it, the philosopher has the happiest life. Happiness will come, not from pleasures, but from the good life itself. In Aristotle's metaphor: "The life of the actively good is inherently pleasant. So their life does not need to have pleasure fastened about it as a necklace, but possesses it as part of itself."[11]

The life of contemplation, Aristotle said, is "too high" for a human being as such. It is possible only because "something divine" is present in the person. He concludes, "The life according to reason is best and pleasantest, since reason more than anything else is human. This life therefore is also the happiest."[12] The life of contemplation, he adds, "seems to need external equipment but little." Oh, *some* "external prosperity" will be needed; human beings do have a body that needs nourishment and "other attention," but "many things or great things" will not be needed for contemplation; "even with moderate advantages [Aristotle said], one can act virtuously."[13]

Thus, though Plato and Aristotle agreed that the life of contemplation and reason enjoyed by the philosopher is the best life, Aristotle contributed the requirement that happiness is active, the exercise of a human being's most essential and defining characteristic. And he admitted both that some material conditions were essential to happiness and that happiness could be damaged or destroyed by the intervention of cruel circumstances. Happiness, for Aristotle, is necessarily more vulnerable than it is for Plato; it is still—as for Plato—a highly individual achievement.

Plotinus, it is well to remember, did not see himself as a "Neoplatonist," but simply as a faithful interpreter of Plato. He inherited several fundamental problems noticed in Plato's teachings by philosophers like Aristotle, and addressed himself to exploring and explaining those problems. He also worked and thought in a different world than that of his predecessors. By Plotinus' time, Christianity, in its many forms, competed with the philosophical schools to provide the most cogent account of human existence and fulfillment. Plotinus' only polemical treatise is *Enneads* 2.9, "Against the Gnostics." He criticized Gnostics for alleging that the created world of bodies and material substances was the evil creation of an evil Creator. He acknowledged that some of their ideas came from certain Platonic suggestions, but he accused them of ignoring and misunderstanding Plato on some crucial points. The logical conclusion of Gnostic teaching, he wrote, is to desire to be put to death so that one can enjoy the life of the mind without physical encumbrances.[14] He tells a parable:

> Two people inhabit the same stately house; one of them declaims against its plan and its architect, but none the less maintains his residence in it; the other makes no complaint, asserts the entire competency of the architect and waits cheerfully for the day when he may leave it, having no further need of a house: the malcontent

imagines himself to be the wiser and to be the readier to leave because he has learned to repeat that the walls are of soulless stone and timber and that the place falls far short of a true home.[15]

Plotinus suggests somewhat snidely that the Gnostics' complaints assume, and serve to mask, a "secret admiration" for those very "stones."[16] He concludes, "As long as we have bodies we must inhabit the dwellings prepared for us by our good sister the Soul in her vast power of laborless creation."[17] Because the Gnostics carried Plato's disregard for body and material world to its metaphysical conclusion, Plotinus was able to see that such views needed to be explicitly modified. This he set out to do.

Plotinus' own proposal for the happy life is that happiness comes from the recognition of beauty. But this sounds deceptively simple; Plotinus will derive from his definition of the happy life a metaphysics, an ethics, and what we might call a "spirituality." Far from being a simple aesthetic appreciation, the recognition of beauty is a *complex* emotion/intellection, requiring commitment and discipline.

> There must be those who see this beauty by that with which the soul sees things of this sort, and when they see it they must be delighted and overwhelmed and excited much more than by those beauties we spoke of before [i.e., earthly beauties], since now it is true beauty they are grasping. These experiences must occur whenever there is contact with any sort of beautiful thing, amazement, and a shock of delight and wonder and passion and a happy excitement. . . . You feel like this when you see, in yourself or in someone else, greatness of soul, a righteous life, a pure morality, courage . . . the one who sees them cannot say anything except that they are what really exists. What does "really exist" mean? That they exist as beauties.[18]

Since recognition of the beautiful is the primary activity that creates human happiness, Plotinus said, "all our toil and trouble is for this, not to be left without a share in the best of visions. The one who attains this is blessed . . . the one who fails to attain it has failed utterly."[19] Plato had similarly identified the goal of rational exercise as a vision of the beautiful. For Plotinus, as for Plato, identifying the beautiful was difficult and elusive. In Plato's treatise on beauty, the *Greater Hippias*, he set out to find, "not what seems to the many to be beautiful, but what is so." Yet at the end of the treatise he is forced to admit, as the only fruit of his search: "So Hippias, . . . I seem to myself to know what the proverb means that says, 'The beautiful things are difficult.'"[20]

Because the perception of beauty defines human happiness, misjudgments about what is the beautiful are the greatest human danger. Because "we are what we desire and what we look upon," the formative effects of contemplation of beauty are crucial to human happiness. Thus, Plotinus endeavored to elucidate a *method* for achieving the vision of beauty that revises Plato's method:

> And what does this inner sight see? When it is just awakened it is not at all able to look at the brilliance before it. So that the soul must be trained first of all to look at beautiful ways of life: then at beautiful works, not those which the arts produce, but the works of those who have a name for goodness: then look at the souls of the people who produce the beautiful works. How, then, can you see the sort of beauty that a good soul has? *Go back into yourself* and look; and if you do not yet see yourself beautiful, then, just as someone making a statue which has to be beautiful cuts away here and polishes there till he has given his statue a beautiful face, so you must cut away the excess and straighten the crooked and clear the dark and make it bright, and never stop working on your statue until the divine glory of virtue shines out on you. . . . If you have become like this, and see it, and are at home with yourself in purity, with nothing hindering you from becoming in this way one, with no inward mixture of anything else, but wholly yourself, nothing but true light: when you see that you have become this, then you have become sight; you can trust yourself then: you have already ascended and need no one to show you: concentrate your gaze and see. This alone is the eye that sees the great beauty. . . . For one must come to the sight with a seeing power made akin to what is seen. You must first become all god-like and all beautiful if you expect to see God and beauty.[21]

While Plato's method consisted of abstracting the quality of beauty from the many objects and practices that exhibit it, Plotinus' method entailed a systematic movement from attention to external things to work on an inner life of subjectivity.

It is important to note that, for Plotinus, the primary effects of recognized beauty are *ethical*, not aesthetic: "beautiful works" are "not those produced by the arts," but "the works of those who have a name for goodness." Moreover, the one who has "become sight" understands intimately the *connectedness* of sentient beings, the basis of ethical feeling and activity:

> It must, no doubt, seem strange that my soul and that of any and everybody else should be one thing only: it might mean my feelings being felt by someone else, my goodness another's too, my desire her desire, all our experience shared with each other and with the one universe, so that the very universe itself would feel whatever I feel. We are in sympathetic relation to one another, suffering, overcome at the sight of pain, naturally drawn to forming attachments; and all this can be due only to some unity among us.[22]

Plotinus himself did not write about how he translated this ethical vision into concrete practices. But Porphyry, his biographer, reports that Plotinus was a vegetarian, that he took into his home numerous orphans, conducted business of his own, and taught while maintaining a virtually invulnerable inner recollectedness.[23]

In Plotinus the direct apprehension of the connectedness of the universe is the quintessential human activity, *the* knowledge it would be tragic to miss. The *experience*, through contemplation, of the concrete organic unity of the world requires the integration of intelligence and feeling; it is participation in Beauty:

> But if someone is able to turn around . . . he will see God and himself and the All; at first he will not see *as* the All but then, when he has nowhere to set himself and determine how far he himself goes, he will stop marking himself off from all being and will come to the All without going out anywhere, but remaining there where the All is set firm.[24]

The Great Beauty "makes its lovers beautiful and lovable."[25] Moreover, bodies are not excluded from Plotinus' vision of beauty; rather, "the beauty of beautiful bodies is by participation in the Great Beauty."[26]

II

I have given a rather extended description of Greek thinkers on human happiness partly because I, like many Christian authors who have studied them, find them striking and beautiful. Also, mystical spirituality, although never a prominent feature of biblical Christianity, was so very influential within the history of Christianity. We will consider next one of the most influential of the Christian authors who adopted and adapted Greek versions of human happiness, Augustine, bishop of Hippo in Roman North Africa at the beginning of the fifth century. Like his classical predecessors, Augustine was preoccupied with the *beata vita*, the "happy life" (the title of his first treatise as a Christian). The theme weaves throughout his long career as author and preacher. He once said in a sermon:

> Everyone, whatever his condition, desires to be happy. There is no one who does not desire this, and each one desires it with such earnestness that it is preferred to all other things; whoever, in fact, desires other things, desires them for this end alone . . . in whatever life one chooses . . . there is no one who does not wish to be happy.[27]

Augustine reworked the ideas of happiness that he received from Greek thought in two dramatic and decisive ways. First, he described happiness as fundamentally unattainable in this life, postponing its actualization to another time and space, outside present human experience. He identified the fulfillment of human happiness as the integration of person that would occur in the promised resurrection of the body. Until then, under the fragile and flawed conditions of human existence, nothing but momentary "glimpses" of happiness would be available. His insistence that happiness is not complete until the human body is fully integrated is a reworking of Greek authors' worry about the extent of vulnerability that can be incorporated in a happy life. Yet it also asserts the centrality of body to human being. No Greek thinker was willing to bear the *expense* of this intransigent proposal: postponing human happiness to an afterlife in which the body would be invulnerable to accident, disease, suffering, and death. Augustine was the first expositor of happiness to insist that it has something crucial to do with the body, that the realization of happiness cannot occur until body is rescued from mortality and vulnerability.

Augustine's second revision of classical ideas of human happiness was to describe present experiences of happiness as perpetually and irreducibly in motion, oscillating between poles of desire and delight. For Augustine, desire was a matter of survival, the act of self-identification of the hungry heart. For the soul, he said, is informed and shaped by the objects of its habitual attention and affection, by its desire and delight. He pictured a human self as plastic, composed and articulated by what it loves, stretches toward, and identifies with. To love the fragile fleeting objects and people in the world as if they could provide a total stimulus, a reason for being, then, is to make (quite literally) a deadening choice. When the objects vanish into thin air, so does the soul identified with, and defined by, them.[28] It is, then, a matter of survival for the soul to attach itself with desire and delight to a totally trustworthy object, an object that cannot die.

If "real" happiness is not to be found in this life, how can it even be sought? For Augustine believed that the happy life can be neither imagined nor experienced vicariously. It must somehow be identified in one's own experience if one is to find the energy to move in its direction. In short, an idea of the happy life must be collected from memories of individual personal joy. *Any joys will do,* "base joys and disgraceful things," as well as "good and worthy joys."[29] Once one has gathered composite memories of happiness and constructed from this collection a cumulative memory of what happiness is, then one has something both personal and concrete to *desire,* to long toward. Ultimately, of course, though one must perforce begin with memories of any old joys, it is joy in truth that energizes the happy life: "Certainly the happy life is joy in you, who are truth," he wrote, addressing God.[30]

For Augustine, happiness was not, in this life, a stable possession but a dynamic and a *process.* Its intensity—its delicate beauty—is predicated on its instability, its preciousness linked to its fragility. Yet Augustine also deeply distrusted happiness *now.* At least when he spoke as a theologian, he preferred suffering because one could *learn* from it. Present happiness is deceptive; it cannot last forever. And permanence was one of Augustine's requirements for true happiness—not merely the lifelong happiness Aristotle required for happiness worthy of the name, but *eternal happiness.*

Augustine's heady notion of eternal happiness has had its effects in the history of Christianity. His requirement that happiness worthy of the name is necessarily permanent eventuated in centuries of Christians who neither anticipated nor valued happiness now. They expected work and suffering; that is what they recognized as validating their Christianity. Too often in the history of Christianity, happiness was devalued to the point described by Thomas à Kempis in his fifteenth-century best-selling devotional manual, *The Imitation of Christ*. Human happiness, for Thomas, was limited to the security of being well prepared for death:

> A man is not only happy but wise also, if he is trying, during his lifetime, to be the sort of man he wants to be found at his death. We can be sure of dying happily if our lives show an utter disregard for the world, a fervent desire for progress in virtue, a love of discipline, the practice of penitence, denial of self, and acceptance of any adversity for the love of Christ.[31]

Curiously, Augustine's overvaluation of happiness, his demand that it be a permanent state, his investment in sheltering it from the vulnerability of human life, have denied the possibility of "enough happiness," a "working happiness," a humanly achievable happiness. Moreover, the voluntary relinquishment of happiness in "this life" did not inspire committed work for just societies, only for individual salvation.

III

I must now "deliver", as promised, my own reconstruction of inherited conceptualizations of human happiness. I confess initially that, of the authors I have described, I can work most fluently with Plotinus' description of happiness. I need, however, to correct its individualism and its lack of systematic attention to just social arrangements. I want to modify its intellectualism by proposing that vigorous, committed action in the world can equally be a method for recognizing and augmenting the Great Beauty. In addition, I am committed to Aristotle's willingness to accept the condition of vulnerability in caring for people and objects that can—indeed *will*—eventually be lost. There are also features of Augustine's theory of happiness—its dynamism, its sensitivity to human suffering, for example—that I cannot jettison.

I will begin by asking what values, or "worths,"[32] are placed centrally in a particular theory of happiness. I assume that each theory of happiness endeavors to include and arrange all humanly desirable goods, to show how each "fits" in relation to others. Even Plato included bodily beauty as the *starting point* of his method of ascent to the vision of "beauty itself." Furthermore, each theory of happiness must show how human "goods" should be ordered in notoriously short and unstable human lives, lives that do not have the luxury of the gods who banquet in unthreatened leisure on Olympus.

We can agree immediately, I hope, that the activity of rationality has not been ignored in classical accounts of the happy life. Indeed, reason has been rather thoroughly defended as the core human happiness. In Augustine, of course, rationality was displaced by affectivity or the will as it leans out in self-defining love, either toward God or toward the "city" of this world. This alone would make Augustine a theologian rather than a philosopher. But even Augustine did not "dethrone" reason to the extent claimed by some of his commentators. He still considered rationality the "highest" single capacity of human beings, and he placed it above concern for human society or care for one's own and others' bodies. In short, in all the theories we have considered, two human "goods" are consistently marginalized; they are not articulated in thrilling prose but hastily gathered as afterthoughts. These entities are living bodies and a just society.

As we have seen, Augustine gave human bodies such importance that he refused to imagine a human happiness without invulnerable and permanent bodies, but the cost of this was to exclude the possibility of real happiness *now*. And when the philosophers and theologian we have considered sought to envision humanly good *societies* they either described utopias (like Plato's Republic), or a frankly nonexperiential heavenly city (like Augustine's).

Greek philosophers, like Augustine after them, understood human nature as thoroughly *social*; but they declined to envision happiness as social, as dependent on equality and mutuality in social arrangements, and on just institutions. Augustine could—and did, in great detail—imagine a glorious time of fulfillment and perfection for humanity in the resurrection of the body.[33] Yet even in heaven, he said, rewards will be unevenly distributed. The only difference Augustine envisioned from the heavily stratified city of this world will be that people with less reward will, in the heavenly city, be *content*. In fact, when I examine Augustine's model of permanent happiness, I see how utterly and transparently dependent it is on the "foretastes" or "glimpses" of happiness he knew. Because he had neither envisioned nor worked toward just social arrangements, he could not imagine with any concreteness the society of the heavenly city where, as he acknowledged, "all injustice will disappear and God will be all in all."[34]

Something like Plotinus' description of the connectedness of living things in a vast—and beautiful—universe of interdependence is needed to challenge the individualistic and futuristic salvation of Christian tradition. As Plotinus put it, "there is no place to draw a limit, to say, 'this and no further is I.'" The primary self-identity of a person must be with the universe seen as beauty, as a finely textured relationship of parts to whole in which none of the parts could be without the whole. Moreover, something like Aristotle's notion that happiness is an *activity*, *the* activity most characteristic of human beings, is necessary in order to overcome the potential quietism of contemplation of the beautiful. What if participation in the Great Beauty were to be understood as activity in the world of bodies and society rather than as a self-isolating activity of spiritual exercise?

Until the second half of the twentieth century, people have not been able to identify and to map with scientific precision the interconnectedness of living beings. Plotinus' notion of an interdependent web of sentient and non-sentient entities has been intuited rather than demonstrated, a romantic notion. The intuition has been represented by a long tradition of authors who have frequently been labeled "soft," or "nature worshippers," by a succession of "hard-headed" philosophers. But I suggest that a sea change for thought has occurred in our time, brought about by the scientific capacity to measure, and the technological capability to demonstrate, the tangible and intimate effects of such environmental crises as the disappearance of rain forests, the extinction of animal species, pollution of air, water, and food; the list could go on and on. We consider these situations with alarm, but what is needed to energize our committed work on behalf of bodies and the earth is that we recognize the import of all the news *together*. The universe is utterly interdependent. This knowledge is no longer intuited or romantic, but factual and concrete, *the* fundamental fact of life.

If the universe is irreversibly interconnected for damage, it is also interwoven through veins of energy and delight. Thus, what must be discovered if one is to be happy, now and here, is the broader generosity of the universe, the continuous, amazing circulation of gifts, of love, of light. And this discovery must become the centerpiece of one's identity so that one actually *feels* a part of this circulation of wealth. One's own family is seldom the perfect family to meet one's needs and wants; even chosen friends and lovers are not the right ones, at least for much of the time. And yet, there *is* in the world the very love, light, and plentitude one needs. It is there, circulating through living beings—vivid now in one, now in another. It is not gone from the world when it is gone from me. And knowing it is here, in motion, is enough. In a moment of overwhelming insight, the protagonist in Camus's *L'Etranger* says, "Je m'oeuvre pour le premier fois a la tendre indifference du monde" ("I opened myself for the first time to the gentle nonchalance of the world").

People know this on some level. It is the most evident open secret of the universe. There is music that can make one briefly, perfectly, happy. Many novels come to resolution when their characters discover that there is enough, and that they can find ways to participate in it, that they may finally abandon the effort to extract what they need from their lovers and families. This is also, I think, what Augustine meant when he said, "Cessavi de me paululum" ("I relaxed a little from myself"). The world contains enough, and the perception of this comes as an awareness of beauty, a relaxing. Poetry regularly marks it; Rainier Maria Rilke said:

> And we, who have always thought of happiness climbing, would feel the emotion that almost startles when happiness falls.[35]

In our own century, Alfred North Whitehead was one of the most articulate expositors of the interconnectedness of the universe: he refers in the concluding pages of *Adventures of Ideas* to

> a broadening of feeling due to the emergence of some deep metaphysical insight, unverbalized and yet momentous in its co-ordination of values. Its first effect is the removal of the stress of acquisitive feeling arising from the soul's preoccupation with itself. . . . It is primarily a trust in the efficacy of beauty. . . . [36]

Even fans of media stars know that the fame, beauty, and money the star has collected are—both symbolically and concretely—theirs. They take pleasure in participating in what the star crystallizes and displays for them. The star's social *function* is to demonstrate the existence of *so much*.[37]

What is finally required for happiness is faith in the immense generosity of the universe, experienced as beauty. There is "enough," enough for all, if we will only cease trying to stipulate and control the channels through which it may flow to us, if we will "await it with confidence, and accept it with gratitude."[38] This is not blind faith; it is grounded in vision and in the experience of many witnesses.

Interconnectedness, then, is a scientifically demonstrable fact as well as a feature of experience, but we seldom notice it. Yet there is something abundantly and compellingly energizing in those moments when we see the interconnectedness, what Plotinus calls the "unity," the interdependence of the universe. If, as I have claimed, happiness depends on intimate knowledge and experience of the consanguinity of living beings, then happiness is an art of perception, the vision of an eye that can, and must, be cultivated. Not a vision of the heavenly city; not that of an imagined utopia. But now. Here. Bodied and social. Happiness as desire and delight, delight and desire, in motion, *active* in the world.

We must, however, still ask: what is the relationship between happiness and social arrangements? If happiness is identical with seeing/participating in the Great Beauty, isn't activity antithetical to it? Twentieth-century people often assume that while one is absorbed in "seeing" one is not acting, not struggling to make the world and human society a better place to live for more human beings. Are contemplation of beauty and struggle for social change inevitably alternative postures toward the world? It is important to note that the metaphor of vision does not necessarily imply that the one seeing must be at a distance from the object seen, as some twentieth-century theorists of vision have claimed. Plato was the first to articulate a theory of physical vision that emphasized the viewer's activity and the connection of viewer and object. The visual ray theory states that a quasi-physical ray, created by the same fire that animates and warms the body, is at its most intense in the eyes. The act of vision occurs when the visual ray is directed to an object, *touches its object*, and the object travels back along the ray to imprint itself on the memory. Ancient and medieval folk beliefs about the evil eye, in which a malign look can cause physical and/or spiritual damage, rely on this model of vision as *touch*. The look, then, depends on the actualization of a connection between viewer and object, on the viewer's recognition of this connection and on her/his activity in establishing it. The visual ray theory did not emerge from an entertainment culture, a culture that thinks of seeing as passive; rather it assumes vigorous engagement with the object of vision.

Reliance on a vast unifying vision of beauty can be—and has been—dangerous in ways recently pointed out by twentieth-century philosophers and theologians. Liberation theologians and feminist philosophers and theologians have especially detected the capacity of beauty to blind people—even those who are themselves marginalized or oppressed—to social and institutional injustice. These theologians, righteously angry at unjust political and social arrangements, at oppressions based on race, class, and gender, have often sought to expose and jettison the beautiful texts, liturgies, ideas, and images that masked injustice. Clearly, articulations of beauty must be scrutinized and the ancient Grail question brought to them, "Whom does it serve?" Happiness, then, will require both an energizing and compelling vision of an intimately interconnected world as the site of the "real self," and continuous investigation and revision of the ways this vision is lived in "human, all too human societies."

If happiness, as Aristotle said, is an activity, and if it is, furthermore, an activity that flows spontaneously from our most fundamental gift, our aliveness, then participation in the Great Beauty cannot be confined to the intellectual vision of philosophers. And the life of the philosopher may not be the happiest human life, despite consensus on this among the masters of language.

Let us recall, in conclusion, the Greek anxiety over establishing a site for human happiness that is safe from threat—safe space. How vulnerable to contingencies—events, social arrangements, chance opportunities or the lack thereof—is human happiness? By *human* happiness I mean "enough" or "working" happiness as opposed to "ideal" or "fantasy" happiness. In Plotinus' generous vision, personal or individual vulnerability does not preclude the happiness that is inherent in seeing the great beauty. He did not, however, articulate quite so clearly that the important and irreducible vulnerability in an interconnected universe is transpersonal. But awareness of this kind of vulnerability can be put to work as energy for love and for work. Energized by "the eye that sees the great beauty," one recognizes simultaneously that the condition of vulnerability and the condition of the circulation of gifts are the same—interconnection, the Great Beauty.

NOTES

1. Martha C. Nussbaum, *The Fragility of Goodness: Luck and Ethics in Greek Tragedy and Philosophy* (Cambridge: Cambridge University Press, 1986).

2. Ibid., pp. 2–3.

3. Ibid., p. 5.

4. Ibid., p. 7.

5. Ibid., p. 176.

6. Plato *Symposium* 211 (trans. Benjamin Jowett).

7. Ibid.

8. Ibid.

9. Wallace Stevens, "Sunday Morning," *The Collected Poems of Wallace Stevens* (New York: Alfred A. Knopf, 1978), p. 69.

10. Nussbaum, *The Fragility of Goodness*, p. 369.

11. Aristotle *Nicomachean Ethics* 1.8 (trans. J. A. K. Thomson).

12. Aristotle *Nicomachean Ethics* 10.7 (trans. W. D. Ross).

13. Ibid., 10.8.

14. Plotinus *Ennead* 2.9.17 (trans. A. H. Armstrong).

15. Ibid.

16. "But perhaps they may say that they are not moved, and do not look any differently at ugly or beautiful bodies; but if this is so, they do not look any differently at ugly or beautiful ways of life, or beautiful subjects of study; they have no contemplation, then, and hence no God. For the beauties here exist because of those first beauties. If, then, these here do not exist, neither do those. . . . But one should notice that they should not give themselves airs if they despised something ugly; they do so because they despise something which they begin by calling beautiful: and what sort of a way of managing is that?" (ibid).

17. Ibid.

18. Plotinus *Ennead* 1.6.4 (trans. A. H. Armstrong).

19. Ibid., 1.6.7.

20. Plato *Greater Hippias* 304e; trans. Thomas L. Pangle, *The Roots of Political Philosophy: Ten Forgotten Socratic Dialogues* (Ithaca, N. Y.: Cornell University Press, 1987), p. 339. See also *Republic* 435c, 497d; *Cratylus* 348a–b; *Protagoras* 339ff.

21. Plotinus *Ennead* 1.6.9.

22. Ibid., 4.9.3.

23. "He used to work out his design mentally from first to last; when he came to set down his ideas he wrote out at one spurt all he had stored in mind as though he were copying from a book. Interrupted, perhaps, by someone entering on business, he never lost hold of his plan; he was able to meet all the demands of the conversation and still keep his own train of thought clearly before him; . . . he never looked over what he had previously written, but he linked on what was to follow as if no distraction had occurred.

"Thus he was able to live at once within himself and for others; he never relaxed from his interior attention unless in sleep, and even his sleep was kept light by an abstemiousness that often prevented him from taking as much as a piece of bread, and by this unbroken concentration upon his highest nature" *(Porphyry* Life 8 [trans. A. H. Armstrong]).

24. Plotinus *Ennead* 6.5.7.

25. Ibid., 1.6.7.

26. Ibid., 1.15.

27. Augustine *Sermons* 306.3.

28. Augustine's idea of soul/self could be expressed in a twentieth-century language of the psyche: "The ego is the cumulative effect of its formative identifications. . . . Identifications not only *precede* the ego, but the identificatory relation to the image establishes the ego. . . . As a result the ego is not a self-identical substance, but a sedimented history of relations which locate the center of the ego outside itself, in the externalized *imago* which confers and produces bodily contours" (Judith Butler, "The Lesbian Phallus and the Morphological Imaginary," *Differences* 4:1 [Spring 1992], p. 148).

29. Augustine *Confessions* 10.21 (trans. Rex Warner).

30. Ibid., 10.23.

31. Thomas à Kempis, *Imitation of Christ*, trans. Betty I. Knott (London: Fontana, 1963), p. 73.

32. My colleague, Richard R. Niebuhr, prefers this term.

33. Augustine *De civitate dei* 22 (trans. Henry Bettenson).

34. Ibid., 19.15.

35. Rainer Maria Rilke, *Duino Elegies* 10; trans. J. B. Leishman and Stephen Spender (New York: Norton, 1963), p. 85.

36. A. N. Whitehead, *Adventures of Ideas* (New York: Macmillan, 1933), pp. 283–84.

37. Interestingly, one of Madonna's recent commentators has claimed the social function of stars is to "fill the space of desire—this gap that constitutes the subject in desire for an object" (E. Ann Kaplan, *"Madonna Politics: Perversion, Repression, or Subversion? Or Masks and/as Mastery,"* in *The Madonna Connection*, ed. Cathy Schwichtenberg [San Francisco: Westview Press, 1993], p. 152).

38. Isak Dinesen, "Babette's Feast," *Anecdotes of Destiny* (New York: Vintage, 1974), p. 60.

Blessedness

HUSTON SMITH

I. PRELIMINARY OBSERVATIONS

To set the stage for blessedness, I shall begin with a few First Platitudes about its wider genus, happiness.[1]

A. Happiness is a polar concept. It comes paired with its opposite, unhappiness.

B. Human life oscillates between these poles like a living vibrator. We wouldn't survive without pain receptors that prompt us to remove our hands from hot stoves and are relieved when we do so. Happiness and unhappiness simply generalize this pain-and-its-cessation polarity without which life is inconceivable.[2] If anyone wants to challenge this by claiming that there is a category of beings—enlightened beings or *jīvan-muktas*—who rise above mood swings to a condition of uninterrupted bliss, they should listen to someone who knows what she is talking about, Theresa of Avila, whom I paraphrase as follows: "If anyone were to tell me that he has reached a state of unwavering joy, I would answer that he understands neither what he says, nor who it is that says it."

I am ticking off these first three points as platitudes, but if we were to look beneath their descriptions for explanations—in this instance, *why* life is stretched on these polarities—complications would instantly bristle. Theologians say that pain is a part of life because the world is not God. Not being *nirvana*, *samsāra* cannot in principle be unmitigated *ānanda*; to wish, therefore, that the cosmogonic unfolding outside of God could be operated solely by joy, in joy, and for joy is to violate the laws of logic. Once that fact is accepted, it is possible to see that tribulations can and should prompt growth. "Grief and perturbation bring life, whereas prosperity and pleasure bring death," Mencius tells us.[3] I shall say no more about these themes. Happiness is a roomy subject, and I must stay on course.

C. Pain can be profitably courted to learn from it; down that road lies an entire ascetic theology, but it is a special and treacherous case which I shall bypass for my third platitude: It is masochistic to court pain for its own sake, and normal and healthy to move away from it. But this introduces a tricky point. If we make pain's opposite—happiness—our life objective, we miss it. This is the famous hedonistic paradox of the ethicists which received its classic formulation in Jesus' words: "Whosoever will save his life shall lose it" (Matt. 16:25). In one sense it is easy to unlock this paradox, for happiness increases as we break out of our "skin-encapsulated egos" which are programmed for *taṅhā*: grasping and seeking. But this only seems to settle the matter, for if the paradox is pursued, it opens onto the final mysteries of God and the world. This is why I have chosen blessedness as the species of happiness I want to focus on: I hope to show that blessedness is happiness in its quintessentially paradoxical mode.

It was the chance to explore this paradoxical feature of blessedness that led me to choose it for my topic, but there was an occasioning cause that first suggested the topic to me. Shortly after I was invited to lecture in the series from which this book has emerged, while I was still wondering what aspect of happiness to address, the Beatitudes in a new translation turned up as the Gospel reading in the church I attend. What greeted my ears that Sunday morning was: "*Happy* are the poor in spirit, for theirs is the kingdom of heaven. *Happy* are those who mourn, for they will be comforted. *Happy* are the meek, for they will inherit the earth," and so on. I winced, recalling the morning Robert Schuller came on the Today Show to plug his new book, *The Be (Happy) Attitudes*. That's cute, but I'm not sure that much else can be said for it. We all know the rationale for such tinkerings with scripture, and mostly I'm against it, sensing debasement of verbal currency at work. Beatitude is not happiness. It is a distinct kind of happiness—one that is more momentous than the other modes of happiness. To overlook this is like identifying Mount Everest as a mountain, nothing more.

What, then, is distinctive about blessedness? Let me move toward my answer by distinguishing it from several species of happiness that it can be contrasted with. Mine is not the only way the happiness pie can be cut, but my slices can begin to outline the edges of blessedness by indicating what lies on their other sides.

II. A RUDIMENTARY TYPOLOGY

1. To begin with, blessedness is not *pleasure*, for pleasure seems like the appropriate word for enjoyments that derive from our senses. We speak of pleasurable sensations, and that sounds right. As a young man I read an essay by Rose McCauley titled "Warm Bath," and my muscles still relax when I recall her voluptuous description. Carlos Castaneda locates the epicenter of indulgence in the hot tubs of the Esalen Institute, and pleasure does seem to have an indulgent aspect. A good meal when you are ravenous, the first gulp of fresh air after you've been in a stuffy room, feeling your muscles relax when you climb into bed after a tiring day—such are the pleasures of life, as we appropriately say.

2. My second species of happiness I shall call happiness-in-quotation-marks ("happiness") to distinguish it from the generic sense the word serves in the title of this book. Happiness in my restricted sense differs from pleasure in that pleasures derive from one's body—its sense receptors—whereas happiness is a field phenomenon that characterizes the self in relationship. Typically this relationship is with people, so friendship figures prominently in happiness. Several years ago there was an advertisement for Budweiser beer that enjoyed a considerable run. It featured a summertime backyard barbecue with friends, all handsome, healthy, good-looking, and in good spirits; it played on the standard American dream and was captioned, "This Bud's for you." Beer commercials are as low as one can scrounge for an example of happiness, but the logic extends right up to Aristotle, who placed friendship first among what he calls the external aids to happiness. That it is an important aid goes without saying, but that it heads the list of aids can be questioned; for I know individuals who are happier with nature than with people. In either setting, though, the feeling carries overtones of contentment through at-one-ment, the sense of needing (at the time) nothing more, of experiencing no lack.

3. I mentioned that as much as Aristotle valued friendship, he regarded it as only an external aid to happiness. Happiness in its consummate human form—I shall return to that qualifier "human"—he called *eudaimonia*. I, for my part, will call it *joy*. *Eudaimonia*, for Aristotle, arises from the full functioning of the highest distinctive human faculty, which he took to be reason, or contemplation. Because thought is the distinctive and crowning human excellence, the

power by which humans surpass and rule other forms of life, it stands to reason, Aristotle believed, that its expression will fulfill human beings more than any other activity and elicit the highest sense of well-being that they can experience. "That which is proper to each thing is by nature best and most pleasant for each thing; for man, therefore, the life according to reason is best and pleasantest, since reason more than anything else *is* man. This life therefore is also the happiest" (*Nicomachean Ethics* 10.7.4–7).

I think we all sense something right in what Aristotle says here, and he may be completely right if we read his *nous* generously enough.[4] But the words that are usually used to translate *nous*, namely "reason" or "contemplation," are too cerebral for me to accept as the kingpin of what I am calling *joy*. When Aristotle says categorically that "perfect happiness is a contemplative activity" (*Nicomachean Ethics* 10.8.8), in English at least that is too restricted. With Aristotle, I want to use *joy* for the sensation that surges through us when we are doing especially well what we are especially good at doing, for it is then that we are most intensely and actively alive. I think of Flannery O'Connor who, when the students at Agnes Scott College asked her why she wrote, replied, "Because I'm good at it." But I want to honor the *range* of human talents. I suspect that much the same exhilaration that courses through intellectuals when they are excited by ideas surges through musicians and athletes when they are at their best, and through those children who, with astonishing dexterity, turn Double Dutch Jump Rope into a new art form.

To emphasize that cerebration has no monopoly on *joy* as I am using the word, I shall cite John Muir's account of his dog, Stickeen, in an unforgettable episode. On an Alaskan glacier a widening crevasse had stranded the dog and his master, and the escape route required crossing a wall of ice so sheer that Muir had to chisel his way across it. Sensing death, the dog refused for a long time to risk the passage, but with no alternative and after Muir's ardent, incessant coaxing, Stickeen eventually took his life in his hands and trusted himself to such traces of toeholds as he could find. Plastering himself to the icy wall, for twenty minutes he inched his way across it until, with the end in sight—here I tap into Muir's account—"he looked keenly into the series of notched steps and finger-holds I had made, as if counting them, and fixing the position of each one of them in his mind. Then suddenly up he came in a springy rush, hooking his paws into the steps and notches so quickly that I could not see how it was done, and whizzed past my head, safe at last!"

> And now came a scene! "Well done, well done, little boy, Brave boy! I cried, trying to catch and caress him; but he would not be caught. Never before or since have I seen anything like so passionate a revulsion from the depths of despair to exultant, triumphant, uncontrollable joy. He flashed and darted hither and thither as if fairly demented, screaming and shouting, swirling round and round in giddy loops and circles like a leaf in a whirlwind, lying down, and rolling over and over, sidewise and heels over head, and pouring forth a tumultuous flood of hysterical cries and sobs and gasping mutterings. When I ran up to him to shake him, fearing he might die of joy, he flashed off two or three hundred yards, his feet in a mist of motion; then, turning suddenly, came back in a wild rush and launched himself at my face, almost knocking me down, all the time screeching and screaming and shouting as if saying, "Saved! saved! saved!" Then away again, dropping suddenly at times with his feet in the air, trembling and fairly sobbing. Such passionate emotion was enough to kill him. Moses' stately song of triumph after escaping the Egyptians and the Red Sea was nothing to it. Who could have guessed the capacity of the dull, enduring little fellow for all that most stirs this mortal frame? Nobody could have helped crying with him![5]

This is the joy I am thinking of, but remarkable as John Muir's account of it is, I think he goes wrong at one point. Stickeen's incredible antics were not saying, "Saved! saved! saved!" but rather, "I did it! I did it! I did it! It was impossible, but I did it!" If, instead of actively saving himself, Stickeen had been passively rescued, he would not have mounted half the show Muir relates.

That's joy in my typology, and it is a noble experience. But my next and final category, *blessedness*, is even nobler. As I have been following Aristotle, I find it significant that in rereading him for this essay I came upon something in his account that I hadn't noticed before. He too has a category of felicity that outranks *eudaimonia* (what I translate as "joy"). *Eudaimonia* is the highest felicity that is open to human beings, but beyond it stands *makariotes*, typically translated "blessedness," which the gods enjoy and God enjoys supremely.[6] As the blessedness I shall describe also includes a divine component, I welcome Aristotle's general support in the rest of my reflections.

III. BLESSEDNESS

Blessedness differs most conspicuously from the previous modes of positive affect that I have described in being paradoxical. This feature is so central in its makeup that one is tempted to propose "paradoxical happiness" as the definition of blessedness. This ploy will not work, however, because paradoxicality enters happiness long before blessedness is reached. Masochism is pervertedly paradoxical, but healthy happinesses can be paradoxical too. Poets tell us that "the sweetest songs are those that tell of saddest thought" and that "parting is such sweet sorrow"; and everyone has heard *someone* say of a film, "It was wonderful. I cried all the way through it." I shall hold off on what must be added to distinguish blessedness from these other modes of paradoxical happiness and note here only that the latter are foothills from which blessedness ascends. It is in the Beatitudes that the paradoxes of happiness receive their starkest formulation, so in pursuing this feature I will use them as my reference point as I proceed.

Of the eleven beatitudes that are enumerated in Matthew 5, six are paradoxical. Knowing that beatitude is a form of happiness, we are startled to learn—or would be if we had not grown up with the assertions—that it is the poor, the sorrowful, the insignificant, the hungry and thirsty, the reviled, and the persecuted who are blessed.

If we stop to consider the matter, those claims are astonishing, even astounding. They are an affront to human understanding. The peace that comes to us when we are hungry and find food; when we are lonely and find a friend; when we are sick and feel our strength returning—*those* happinesses are understandable. But blessedness comes in opposite circumstances. It is the peace that visits us—*can* visit us; there's nothing inevitable about it—when we are hungry and no food arrives; when we are lonely and no friend appears; when we fall ill and learn that recovery won't happen. It is the peace that comes shimmering on the crest of a wave of pain; the spear of frustration transformed into a shaft of light. It comes when life has us by the throat; when all options are frozen and there is no escape from the circumstance that bids well to crush us. It may be the death of a child, or an incurable disease, or the onset of blindness. Such things happen. They make us wish that life were different, that it would approach us in a different guise. But it hasn't, and we have no choice but to cope with the fact that has become our identity, our fact.

The peace that comes to us in circumstances like those is the peace that *passeth* understanding, and of course nothing is going to change that. Still, I do want to ponder the matter, so the balance of my statement will proceed as follows: I shall begin by distinguishing two modes of blessedness. Then, moving from phenomenology to ontology, I shall try to offer a bit of an explanation for the most surprising of the two modes I delineate.

IV. TWO MODES OF BLESSEDNESS

Blessedness comes to us in two modes, one of which is proleptic and the other self-contained. We find both modes in the six paradoxical Beatitudes. Four of them are proleptic, cast in the future tense. The sorrowful, the meek, the hungry, and the reviled *are* blessed—present tense, right now—but because of anticipated developments; because at a later date they *will be* comforted, or *will* inherit the earth, or be satiated, or be rewarded. In these cases, the reason we can be happy in the midst of adversity is that we can foresee their end. Our minds can reach out and *appropriate* the future, bringing it to some extent into the present. The news that I will recover from my illness can make me blessed while my body is still in pain.

Proleptic blessedness hinges on faith and hope that a given future will transpire; and when we think of the proportion of our lives that are lived in the light of these twin virtues it may be fitting that twice as many of the paradoxical beatitudes—four as against two—are cast in the proleptic mode. Two, though, are self-contained. In the case of the poor in spirit and those who are persecuted for righteousness' sake, we are told that "theirs *is* the kingdom of heaven." The use of the present tense implies that their happiness doesn't depend on the future. It is self-contained.

For example, when the Massachusetts Institute of Technology imported Robert Graves for three weeks while I was there, departments were invited to host him for suppers, and we philosophers availed ourselves of the opportunity. I will pass over the moment when, dishes having been cleared, Graves pushed back his chair, lit his cigar, and asked, "What do you gentlemen have against ghosts?" causing Hilary Putnam to choke on his brandy. I will pass over that interesting moment to relate something else he said because I want to use it as the first of my two instances of self-contained blessedness. In World War I Graves was with the Royal Fusiliers. One of their number was trapped in a burning tank, but in the nick of time was miraculously rescued. When his buddies commiserated with him for the terror he must have experienced, encased as he had been in sheets of flame, he replied: "On the contrary. I was ecstatic."

David Livingstone reported a similar experience when he was almost mauled to death by a lion, and it is possible that these cases can be explained naturalistically by the endorphins that the brain secretes in such emergencies. There would remain the mystery of how natural selection could have produced this strikingly merciful phenomenon when it occurs at the moment of death and has no survival value, but I won't go into that. Instead, I will proceed to my other example of self-contained blessedness for which I see no prospect of a naturalistic explanation.

This second example comes from a young woman I know. When she described the incident to me shortly after it occurred, I asked her to do me the favor of writing it down and I shall read her account in full.

> On April 28, 1981, after one year of marriage, I was taken by rude surprise when my husband said he might leave me for another woman. It was a blow that seemed to smash my heart to pulp. I was engulfed by rage and grief.
>
> That night I didn't sleep. My adrenalin was pumping its instinctual response to attack. When morning came I sat on the deck of the house and let the hot, blinding sun pour into me. My body felt like a cold, empty shell. Every cell cried out for the renewal, strength, and life-giving warmth of the sun. What I had thought to be a solid foundation upon which to build my life, now appeared as unstable as a turbulent sea. My "reality" was suddenly shown to be illusion. What now could I trust or believe? To find the answer, the deepest core of myself opened and reached out. I faced the sun straight on and cried, over and over, "God help me! God help me! God help me!"
>
> Midday, when I went inside, my eyes fell on *Reflections of the Christ* by David Spangler. I picked it up and read all after-

noon. The words spoke directly to my need. By evening I was feeling strong and calm, though still in shock. My husband asked for a divorce that evening. I cried, but I could feel strength and an enduring truth and light within me.

That night I again lay awake all night, but my spirit felt calmer and deeper. Without purposely meditating, I may have been in a state of deep meditation. After I had been in bed about an hour—it must have been about 11:30 p.m.—a large beam of light seemed to enter the top of my head and extend vertically through my body. I experienced it as a bright shaft of light, six to eight inches in diameter. It was a timeless experience, for I had no thoughts to tick away minutes, but it may have lasted about half an hour. The assurance of a greater reality was given. There may be no anchor to hold, but in time of need, the shaft of light let me know that I am part of the whole. Like a lighthouse, it showed me home, and said "all is well."

Over the next few months, twice more I felt: Oh Lord, help me; this is too much to bear, and I don't understand. From the depths I opened in complete receptivity and strong need. Each time, something like a reflection of the beam of light again connected me to "the heavens," and filled my heart with warmth.

So this was Grace. In a time of deep need it came—an unexpected gift, a blessing.

In my concluding section I want to pass from phenomenology, which describes our experiences, to ontology, which provides the resources we have for explaining them. One cannot prove ontologies from human experience, the world being religiously ambiguous. But occasionally human experiences part the clouds of nescience that Kant considered impenetrable, and I propose to push the possibility that our experience of blessedness offers us reliable insights into the ultimate nature of things.

V. ONTOLOGICAL IMPLICATIONS

In tracking the paradox in blessedness, it is useful to realize that every serious inquiry seems to dead-end in it. In *physics*, relativity and quantum mechanics are so blatantly paradoxical that they drove Niels Bohr to conclude that while the opposite of a small truth is a small error, the opposite of a big truth is another big truth. The *religious* counterparts of frontier physicists are the mystics, and Stace (like all others who study them) concludes that "their kind of consciousness is completely paradoxical."[7] In *philosophy*, Kant found that when concepts are applied to other than empirical entities, contradictions necessarily ensue. And even *logic*, which takes consistency as its *sine qua non*, eventuates in paradox: if the ship's barber is the man who shaves everyone who doesn't shave himself, he both does and does not himself get shaved. Gödel's theorem has the last word.

What are we to make of this fact: that reason everywhere comes to the end of its tether and finds itself confronted with the inconsistency it has to avoid to get as far with its problems as it does? What *I* make of it, and I am of course not alone in this, is that reason, with all its uses, is an inadequate instrument for discerning Reality, the way things finally are. Like our two-dimensional Mercator maps that have their uses but inevitably distort the three-dimensional planet they purport to represent, reason does not and cannot map Reality with full accuracy. So its inaccuracies *must* generate contradictions. At that point, all reason can do is make peace with the effrontery by explaining why both horns of the dilemmas it has generated are required.

If Reality cannot be squeezed into reason's procrustean bed, why should we expect it to fit our emotions? If our minds can't subsume Reality in a glance, what reason is there to expect that a single mood could do it justice? Moods are mercurial. They bob up and down, taking snapshots of life sequentially—now its sunny side, now its shadows. Systematically they circle the Whole, never capturing it except in one, unique, exceptional experience. In blessedness we come close to experiencing the Whole's outlines in one decisive respect. We experience its value antinomies—light and dark, good and evil, joy and sorrow—simultaneously, concurrently, and as reconciled. William James registered this point definitively in his discussion of mysticism: "It is as if the opposites of the world, whose contradictoriness and conflict make all our difficulties and troubles, were melted into unity. Not only do they, as contrasting species, belong to one and the same genus, but *one of the species*, the nobler and better one, *is itself the genus, and so soaks up and absorbs its opposite into itself.*"[8] Augustine made the same point. "I had come to see that higher things are better than the lower, but that the sum of all creation is better than the higher things alone."[9]

These statements contain all the ingredients I need for the definition of blessedness I have been working toward. Blessedness is (a) *paradoxical* in embracing James' "opposites." (b) The nobler of these opposites "absorbs" the other, which makes blessedness paradoxical *happiness*, not paradoxical pain. And, unlike the foothill examples of paradoxicality that I cited earlier—"parting is such sweet sorrow," and the like—(c) the experience of blessedness accurately positions "the opposites *of the world*"; opposites as they figure in the deepest structure of things.

Having at last defined blessedness, I shall conclude by suggesting how theologians should interpret the phenomenon, using the experience of the woman I quoted as my example.

That the shaft of light *came* to her suggests its independent, ontological otherness. It was not an epiphenomenon, conjured by her neurological system in a traumatic state. The forms in which she *clothed* what came—her image of a beam six to eight inches in diameter, and even that it consisted of light—were of her making, but that no more calls into question the independent reality of the X that she apprehended than the independent existence of the Grand Tetons would be challenged by the shifting ways she would see them if she drove through them.

Second, the fact that the Light did for her what she was unable to do for herself—restore her strength and her hope—suggests that it has greater power than she.

And third, that it answered her cry suggests that it is benevolent. In the last half century, psychosomatic medicine has demonstrated that invisible, immaterial realities—thoughts and emotions—can exert "downward causation" on matter to produce somatic effects that range from ulcers to improved immunity systems. The basic religious posit is that beyond our thoughts and emotions there is at least one additional level of reality (I omit here the question of angels) that houses a Being who in ways is distinct from us and is concerned for us. He/She/It is more powerful and compassionate than we are, and its healing power towards us becomes discernible in moments that we called blessed.

If that *is* the classic religious understanding of blessedness, I should like to know two things. First, has science—the only really new incursion in history—discovered anything that renders this straightforward religious reading of the woman's account untenable?

And second, are contemporary theologians willing to endorse the outlines, at least, of that straightforward reading? If not, why not?

NOTES

1. Special thanks to Kendra Smith for her contributions to this essay.

2. On balance human beings seem to manage to maintain an ever-
normal granary of both happiness and suffering. On the debit side of the
equation, *Harper's* Index recently disclosed that the average number of days
that an American is in a bad mood is 110, and that the percentage of Americans who are in a good mood every day is 2 ("Harper's Index," *San Francisco
Chronicle Parade Magazine*, 2 January 1994, p. 6). Another recent study
shows that after the initial depression following a tragedy, or elation following the winning of a sweepstakes, the mood swings of most subjects returned
quite quickly to their earlier patterns.

3. Mencius.

4. See the way I read Aristotle's *nous* in "Educating the Intellect: On
Opening the Eye of the Heart," in *Can Virtue Be Taught?*, ed. Barbara
Darling-Smith (Notre Dame, Ind.: University of Notre Dame Press, 1993).

5. John Muir, *Stickeen* (Reprint, Berkeley: Heyday Books, 1990),
pp. 62-64.

6. The whole life of gods is blessed [and God] . . . surpasses all others
in blessedness" (Aristotle *Nicomachean Ethics* 10.8.25, 22-23).

7. W. T. Stace, *Teachings of the Mystics* (New York: New American
Library, 1960), p. 22.

8. William James, *The Varieties of Religious Experience* (New York:
Macmillan, 1961), p. 306.

9. Augustine *Confessions* 7.8.19.

PART II

Joy, Enlightenment, Humanness

The Inwardness of Joy in Jewish Spirituality

MICHAEL FISHBANE

THE SPIRITUAL FACE OF JUDAISM is drawn from many lines. There are, first and foremost, the biblical sources; a myriad of midrashic inventions; and innumerable works which construct from these materials distinct paths of perfection. These books include the vast philosophical, moral, and mystical literature of Judaism—beginning with such early tracts as *Pirkei Avoth* (the so-called "Ethics of the Fathers"), *Avoth de-Rabbi Nathan*, and *Derekh Eretz*, and including the spiritual guidebooks of Safed and the homilies of Hasidic masters nearer our own day. As the tradition unfolds, biblical phrases combine with rabbinic interpretations into ever thicker ensembles of theological counsel. The old texts are thus compounded and take on new resonance as the legal duties of the *halakhah* are infused with new spiritual dimensions. By the same token the so-called "spirit of the Law" assumes unexpected tones of obligation, and daily worship is instilled with requirements of focused attention. In this way, the externality of the *halakhah* frames inner intentions and an absolutely God-centered piety.

Given all this, we may wonder: how can the theme of *joy* receive its due? How might we coordinate the diverse dicta of the Bible with their applications over three millennia? For if you contend, correctly, that the psalmist's exhortation to "worship God with joy" (Psalm 100:2) means, in context, the joyful celebration of cultic worship, you must still reckon with the expanded sense of divine service (*ʿavodah*) in later Judaism, which includes every aspect of religious action. In this wider context, the old evocation is transformed into a counsel concerning one's proper state during worship. By the same token, the psalmist's ensuing call to "know that the Lord is God" (v. 3) is read by later tradition in terms of the preceding exhortation—such that the sequence of verses suggests a spiritual itinerary of sorts: from (or through) joyous worship to divine wisdom.

In view of this complexity, it would be a barren project indeed simply to collect passages pertinent to our theme and set them out one by one. My aim here is rather to evoke something of the thick texture of joy in Jewish theology, and the dynamic tensions that exist between law and spirit, and the natural and the supernatural. Just here, I believe, is the heartbeat of Judaism. To sharpen our sensibilities, I shall repeat the residue of a Hasidic homily from the early nineteenth century. We may then go back to medieval sources and their retrieval of the ancient rabbinic legacy.

Responding to the biblical verse "And all the nation saw the *voices*" (literally, the "sounds" or "thunderclaps"; Exod. 20:18), Rabbi Moshe Ḥayim Ephraim of Sudilkov (1748–1800) proposed a parable heard from his grandfather, Rabbi Israel Ba'al Shem (founder of modern Hasidism), to resolve the bizarre oxymoron whereby the people apparently saw sounds during the theophany on Sinai. It goes as follows.

> There was once a musician who performed on a very fine instrument with great sweetness and pleasantness (ʿarevut), and all who heard this could not restrain themselves because of the great sweetness and joy and leaped in dance nearly to the ceiling . . . ; and whoever was nearby and came close to hear the instrument had the most pleasure and danced greatly. (Now) amidst the tumult there came a deaf man who could not hear any sound (qol) of the pleasant instrument, but only saw the people dancing mightily and thought them to be mad, musing "What can joy accomplish?" And truly, were he wise and understood that (all) this was due to the great pleasure and loveliness of the instrument's sound he would also have danced then and there. Now the meaning (of the parable) is clear, and one may apply it to the verse, "and all the nation saw the sounds"; that is to say, that God, be He blessed, appeared before all (the people) in the unity of His divine light, which they altogether perceived. For when they saw the great joy (for "the heavenly hosts were rejoicing, etc.") they understood that this was because of the sweetness and loveliness of the light of the holy Torah, and pressed forward to hear the sound (qol) of the Torah, for they were as yet somewhat deaf (for they did not "hear" the sounds). Now all became wise and their eyes were opened; for when they saw the great happiness and joy

(of the angels) they understood that (this was) surely (due to) the sounds, that is to the loveliness and pleasantness of the sound (or Voice) of Torah. (Thus:) even though they did not perceive the (true) loveliness of the Torah, they understood from the joy (expressed by the angels) that this was due to the great loveliness of the Torah—and thus they pressed themselves forward to hear the sound itself, in the hopes that they might yet perceive and understand the loveliness of the light of the Torah. And the enlightened will understand this. (*Degel Maḥaneh Ephraim, Yitro*)

There are several layers to this homily. To begin, let us note a discordance between the opening parable and its subsequent application. In the former, the deaf man retains a negative judgment about joy, and does not achieve any deeper understanding. In the latter, the people first perceive a limited, visual truth, and then penetrate to a deeper comprehension. From this difference we may infer that the parable was formulated independently of the biblical verse and its interpretation. In fact, the Baꜥal Shem's parable was probably originally intended to ridicule the opponents of early Hasidism who aggressively criticized ecstatic antics in prayer. The Hasidic counterthrust here is that such rebuke was utterly devoid of religious insight. The citation from Ecclesiastes ("What can joy achieve?") underscores this jibe—for through it the rebukers are made to condemn themselves as spiritually deaf and able to see only the external or frivolous aspects of joy. Accordingly, the Rabbi of Sudilkov gives the parable a new turn when he applies it to the scriptural verse. For now the nation is shown to transcend an original "deafness" by its ability to see behind the dancing angels to the source of their joy—the holy Torah and the sweet sound of God's word. And if the angelic dance is now transfigured as an act of supernatural joy, so too, we reason, is the dance of true believers an ecstatic expression of transcendence. Indeed, through joy the Hasid may transcend his earthly nature and connect with the inner light of Scripture—whose splendor is a facet of God Himself.

※ ※ ※

The topos of music, dance, and religious joy is an old one, and takes us back to a famous passage in the *Mishneh Torah*, the legal code of Moses Maimonides (1135–1201). In the context of rules pertaining to the feast of Tabernacles, the master discusses joy on the festivals (*Yad Ḥazaqah, hilkhot lulav,* chap. 8, hal. 12). "It is a *mitzvah* (religious obligation) to rejoice" on the festivals, he says, and especially on the feast of Tabernacles, since the Torah requires seven days of celebration "before the Lord." Basing himself on older rabbinic discussions (*Mishnah Sukkah* 5.1–4), Maimonides then goes on to specify the events that took place in the Temple—where there were flutes and lyres, songs and words, and all manner of dancing and leaping in joy (hal. 13). While the philosopher tempers such extreme expressions of joy, and limits them largely to sages and pietists (hal. 14), he owns that joy in the fulfillment of the commandments is required of all. This comprehensive principle is emphasized in the final paragraph of his discussion.

> The joy (*simḥah*) which a person expresses in doing a *mitzvah* and the love of God that He commanded thereby is a great act of worship. And whoever restrains himself from this joy will be requited by God, as is said: "(You will be punished) *because* you have not served your God with joy and good cheer." (Deut. 28:47) . . . (hal. 16)

In this important passage, Maimonides makes clear that the joyful performance of the commandments is an exalted form of worship and an expression of the love of God. In the immediate sequel he goes on to stress that such joy should not be for self-exaltation or aggrandizement. Rather, the commandments should be performed as acts of selflessness and humility "before God." In this way, the wholly natural emotion of joy is transformed through divine service and actualizes the religious love which must motivate the worshipper. This halakhic ideal is reinforced by later commentators who invoke the older Talmudic epigrams which inform Maimonides' ideal. The words of the *Maggid Mishneh* (by Vidal Yom Tov of Tolosa, fourteenth century) are indicative: "(These matters concerning joy) are clarified in several places in the Talmud and in the chapter *bameh madliqin* (*b. Shabbat* 30b), where the sages explained (the verse) 'And I praised joy'—as referring to the performance of the commandments in joy (*simḥah shel mitzvah*). And the principal point here is that a person should not perform the commandments because they are required of him and he is forced and constrained to do them, but he should perform them joyfully and thus do what is good because it is good and what is true because it is true; and he should regard their burden as light in his eyes and understand that he was created thus to serve his creator. . . . (For indeed) the joyful performance of the commandments and the study of Torah and Wisdom is the true joy. . . ."

Roughly contemporary with Maimonides' ideal of joy in the performance of the commandments are various passages in the *Zohar* which point in the same direction, and give a new mystic intensity to several biblical and rabbinic passages. For example, the verse in Psalms, enjoining worshippers to "serve the Lord with fear, [and] *rejoice [before Him] in trembling*" (Psalm 2:11), is now invoked to express caution in earthly pleasures: "For (though) it is forbidden for a human being to rejoice overmuch in this world, or in ordinary words, it is permissible to rejoice (*ba'ei le-mehdi*) in the words of Torah and in the commandments of Torah" (*Aharei Mot* 3.56a–56b). Like its cognates, this interpretation juxtaposes natural joy to its opposite and establishes Torah as a divine source of supernatural activity in this world. Rabbenu Bahye ben Asher, a member of the spiritual conventicle that produced parts of the *Zohar*, makes a similar point—but in an exegetically more audacious way. In his hands, the famous biblical injunction to "be exceptionally (*'akh*) joyous" (Deut. 16:15) on the feast of Tabernacles was dramatically transformed. Using the particle *'akh* in a specialized legal sense, Bahye construed the command to mean that *only* the joy expressed through worship was permitted—never natural pleasure (see his Bible commentary, and *Kad ha-Qemah, simhah, Kitvei R. Bahye*, [ed. Chavel], p. 273). In this way a moderate religious asceticism was advocated, and joy tolerated only in its transfigured forms.

But joy has other powers, and these too are revealed in the *Zohar*. Chief among these powers are the transcendental-mystical effects of religious joy—which may at once repair the feminine divine gradation, called Shekhinah (*Terumah* 2.131b) and induce her heavenly descent to persons and places on earth (*Va-yehi* 1.216a). In the latter case, the text states in the name of R. Yosi: "The Shekhinah only dwells in a complete (or perfected) place—never in a place of lack, or defect, or sadness; (and) only in an upright place, a place of joy. For that reason, all the years that Joseph was separated from his father, and Jacob was sad, the Shekhinah did not dwell within him." In the larger context of the *Zohar*, this comment is hardly a homiletic conceit. Rather does it express the vital theurgic power of joy—a power which leads to divine indwelling and inspiration. This point is even more baldly stated in the rabbinic source (*b. Shabbat* 30b) from which the Zoharic teaching is derived. Following a comment on Eccles. 8:16, which interprets the joy which the Preacher praised to be the joyful performance of commandments, the Talmud adduces another remark from Ecclesiastes (2:2). As formulated, the query "And what does joy achieve?" is presumed to fly in the face of the Preacher's assertion "And I praised joy" (8:16). But this contradiction is easily resolved by applying the first phrase to nonreligious reverie. This done, a larger conclusion is drawn in which these two types of joy are presumed "to teach you that the Shekhinah does not dwell (on earth) amidst sadness (ʿatzvut), or laziness, or folly, or lightheadedness, or (idle) conversation, or worthless matters—but (rather) amidst the joyous performance of a commandment (*simḥah shel mitzvah*), as is said: 'And now, get me a musician' (said the prophet Elisha); and behold as the musician played the hand of the Lord came upon him'" (2 Kings 3:15).

Never mind the seeming *non sequitur* of the conclusion. Note rather the consequential effects of joy adduced here (through the "ʾein . . . ʾela" ["not. . . but"] formula), along with the theurgical tenor of the prooftext—where music induces divine inspiration. In fact, it would seem from the combination of the two statements (joyous performance plus prooftext) that the Talmud conceives religious joy to function something like a musical current—with magnetic powers of attraction. For indeed both effectively cause the divine Presence to descend upon the human being. Gracious divine indwelling is the result in the first case; prophetic inspiration in the second. Given this, one may wonder whether their combination has a more deliberate purpose—namely, to project a correlation between *nomos* and the Holy Spirit. Put differently: might not this passage be an attempt to suggest a popular realization of spiritual powers *through the commandments*—as a counterpoint to more anomistic practices also performed by mystical virtuosi? I am inclined to believe so, and thus see a direct line of continuity between this rabbinic source and later Zoharic notions. But however this be, there are at least two points which distinguish the Talmudic text from its Zoharic reception. The first of these is that the *Zohar* substitutes spiritual defects for the more moral flaws of silliness and sloth adduced by the Talmud as reasons for divine distance. This is thoroughly in accord with its mystical apprehension of sin, and the effect of sin upon the Shekhinah. The second transformation is that the *Zohar* refers to joy generically—as a particular quality of the spiritual life, lived in accordance with the divine commandments. This point will prove especially significant in later literature. But first some broader considerations.

* * *

In the religious materials of the sixteenth century, a remarkable range of works take up the issue of joy in divine worship and focus on its important and transforming effects—particularly over against older ascetical practices and ideals. Especially notable are the discussions of such mystics as Rabbi Eliezer Azikri (in his *Sefer Ḥaredim*), Rabbi Ḥayim Vital (in his *Shaʿarei Qedushah*, Rabbi Moses Alsheikh (in his Torah and Psalms commentary, the *Torat Moshe* and *Rommemut El* respectively), and Rabbi Moshe Cordovero (in his *'Or Neʿerav*). But it is to Cordovero's student, Rabbi Elijah de Vidas, and his massive spiritual-moral compendium *Reshith Ḥokhmah*, that we must turn here. Not only is his discussion of *simḥah* (joy) the most comprehensive among his peers, but his reception of innumerable biblical, rabbinic, and Zoharic dicta is organized in a striking theological-spiritual manner. In fact this stunning conspectus of sources arranges these teachings on several registers, and constructs a spiritual agenda for the adept. No wonder the work won the hearts of later pietists.

The core of de Vidas' discussion on religious joy occurs in Part 2 of *Reshith Ḥokhmah*, the *Shaʿar Ha-'Ahavah* (or "Gate of Love"), Chapter 10 (and all 50 subsections); but substantive points are also made in Chapters 11 (especially secs. 11, 26, and 33) and 12 (notably secs. 20–26). Chapter 10 is the most systematic of these presentations; and while there is no formal breakdown into larger units, it is possible to discern some progression from the divine to the human realms—though the two are never totally separated, and are mystically correlated throughout. This fact emerges at the outset, when the author explains his editorial decision to juxtapose a discussion of joy to the acts required for the mystical-spiritual repair (*tiqqun*) of the Shekhinah, since "all the aforementioned acts, which a person should do for the repair of the Shekhinah, must be done in joy" (chap. 10, sec. 1). De Vidas reinforces his point with two prooftexts from Scripture and a citation of the *Zohar*'s reuse of *b. Shabbat* 30b, discussed earlier. In this way he indicates the double dynamic of religious joy: it not only repairs the Shekhinah in the divine world, but draws her earthward and *into* the celebrant. Joy thus provides the pure energy of religious praxis—repairing the cosmos and producing mystical infusion. It is an act in the natural world with supernatural results.

After this prologue, the author turns his attention to awakening the requisite religious consciousness in the reader, so that the redemptive results might be realized (10.3–14). Contemplation of God's cosmic goodness, expressed through the harmony of the heavenly hosts, is advised first. It not only generates a desire to imitate these beings in their joyous service of God, but to reflect upon the song of the spheres. Psalm 148 provides crucial instruction in this regard. Ostensibly, this hymn merely invokes a hierarchy of hallelujahs— in which all creation is bidden to praise God, from the heavens above to the earth below. Now surely this alone would be a wonderful chorus of song; but the mystical sense of the passage goes further. For in this apprehension the psalm reveals nothing less than the praise of the Cosmic Pleroma, or intra-divine structure. That is to say, each element mentioned in the biblical hymn is decoded as an aspect of the divine Being—such that the span of song from the high heavens to the earth symbolizes the full extent of the Divine Person, from kingly "Crown" to royal "Dominion" (see *Zohar, Pequdei*, 2.232a; cited by de Vidas). Accordingly, the secret of the psalm is that the divine Structure is a concordance of joyful song. Just this is its inner dynamic and wholeness; and just this does the worshipper contemplate in order to activate a similar harmony in the worshipper's own being. The result, on the human plane, is the joyful service of God. Its reciprocal effect is to repair the Shekhinah, and thereby strengthen the supernal songs above.

The awakening of joy through contemplation is the first step of a revived religious consciousness. But it must be sustained—particularly against the sorrows of sin, and the depressive diminishments this breeds. Accordingly, de Vidas turns in the next sequence of passages to those sacral actions which may keep joy alive (10.14–27). He begins with the priestly and levitical powers of Torah study (*simhat ha-Torah*) and song, respectively (cf. *Zohar, Vayiqra*, 3.8a–b); and from there considers the prayers of the synagogue and the joyful fulfillment of the daily commandments. In these various ways the celebrant is infused with radiance and joy, and kindles the upper face(t)s of the divine Being. Holy lights then stream downward and illumine the worshipper with a supernatural aura. This mystery is also enacted through joyful reception of the face of everyone (10.22)—especially one's teacher or a sage, as well as the poor who come as guests to one's table on the feast of Tabernacles. The ethics of everyday life thus provide sacramental situations of supernal significance; for the "every" of *everyone* mystically alludes to the highest Crown; the sage symbolizes the Shekhinah; and the guests constitute other gradations of the Godhead. Life, then, is myth; myth a mystery; and the core of mystery is joy.

De Vidas' discussion of the festival days concludes with reference to the cosmic conjunctions effected by joy—symbolized by the unification of the letters of the divine Name (10.27–28). The discussion provides an effective transition to another means of activating joy in the worshipper: contemplation of the Name and Greatness of God in isolation (*hitboddedut*; 10.28–31). In context, this is a more inward and personal act than the ethical or halakhic practices discussed earlier—though it certainly recalls the initial awakening of divine consciousness and joy mentioned at the beginning of the chapter (10.3ff). It also allows de Vidas the occasion to consider the human transfiguration that results from such meditation (see *Sha'ar ha-Qedushah* 6.9; 7.117–123). For such mystical acts induce a "wondrous radiance, which is (true) joy" that vitalizes the body to a supernatural degree. For indeed, the concordance between the divine Anthropos and its earthly image not only means, first, that every physical enactment of the commandments by the worshipper produces power and pleasure in the Pleroma; but also that every mental activation of the divine Whole stimulates a simultaneous transfer of its supernatural effects to the human self. Such is the mystery and magic of joy.

In the remainder of the chapter de Vidas harks back to earlier themes. First he equates Torah with song, so that both its study and the recitation of praises constitute positive expressions of joy and lead to spiritual cleaving with God (10.32-37; cf. 14–18). This leads to a long parenthesis on the misuse of song and joy, together with cautions concerning frivolity and the temptations of this world (10.38–43; sec. 41). The final sections (10.44–50) return to the positive expressions of joy (like blessing, prayer, and fulfillment of the commandments), together with a reemphasis of the fact that "love and joy are one thing" (10.44; cf. 45). Indeed it is precisely the duty to love God and arouse this love through joyful worship that brings the chapter to its climax (10.46), and links it to a similar emphasis at the outset (10.4). And as a final caveat against despair, de Vidas stresses the need to conquer sadness—which darkens the divine faces on high (10.49). In fact, by this eviction of sorrow the seeker will prepare an inner basis for the influx of God's spirit into the soul (10.49). In this way, too, the author closes his chapter through allusion to its beginning. As there (10.1), sadness restrains the descent of the Shekhinah and joy induces her indwelling in the human heart. The deep psycho-spiritual effects of joy thus pervade the book from start to finish; for as much as de Vidas is concerned with the repair of divine Wholeness, he knows that this cosmic redemption depends upon the personal redemption of each believer. Moreover, through his emphasis on the influx of the Shekhinah as the earthly consequence of joy, our teacher reveals his pietist's passion for unity with God and reception of the Holy Spirit—two themes which pervade sixteenth-century Safed and the circles in which de Vidas moved. His final paragraph reminds the reader that the Shekhinah is yet in exile; and though he must identify with her sadness through tears and travail, this mourning must be purified through joy—and then redemption will dawn and the Light of Heavenly Joy will fill the earth (cf. 10.50).

One might conclude that this is climactic enough. But having put particular stress on the repair of the Shekhinah in Chapter 10, de Vidas turns his focus more directly on the inner life of the person in the ensuing discussions. Herewith he rises to ecstatic descriptions that are illumined by his own inner perfection. Thus, first, in the context of celebrating the purifications of ritual immersion, de Vidas reminds the adept that through joy in the commandments one may cleave to God, be bound to transcendent Life, and perfect his soul (11.33). These three effects are in fact one, and arise from the depths of faith and trust in God (12.20–21). For the flame of love kindled on this altar rises through joyful performance of the commandments into a luminescent transfiguration of the self in God's fire. The highest expression of this devotion is the acceptance in joy of everything that befalls one in this world (12.22). In this way, wholly natural being is transformed by the totalization of joy: for to be joyful in one's lot is not merely a matter of stoic resignation, as one might deduce it from the ideal formulated in the old Ethics of the Fathers; but rather to accept in radiant equanimity the persistence of God's providence, apportioned to him daily (12.23). The depths of joy thus transcend the fruits of this world, and enrich the believer with a divine inheritance. This, finally, is the mystical truth for de Vidas of the psalmist's assertion: "Light is sown for the righteous (*tzaddiq*), and joy to the upright in heart" (Psalm 97:11). For the righteous one, who justifies (*yatzdiq*) God's ways, is sown with the sustenance of heavenly light, even as the hearts of those who resolutely accept the portions of providence are irradiated by joy (12.24). The human soul is then "enlightened by the Light of Divine Life" (Job 33:30), and expands in holy splendor into the sanctuary of God's Truth. In this Holy of Holies the soul sparkles in silent joy, transformed into an angel of God's presence (13.26).

✵ ✵ ✵

William James' wisdom concerning the *Varieties of Religious Experience* contrasts the healthy-minded person, on the one hand, for whom the goodness and divine vitality of existence is an ever-present and dominant feature of consciousness, with the so-called sick soul, who is obsessed by evil and sin—not to mention the fragmentariness of things, as an inner and outer reality. These polar types, being ideal, are thus only pure for the sake of analysis. But perhaps for that very reason these types also permit a widening of the lenses to include other, similar expressions. I have in mind, of course, just those two modes so emphasized and so juxtaposed from Talmudic discussions on: namely, joy and sadness. For like the healthy-minded type, the structure of joy as a religious modality is characterized by bountiful devotion and inclusive vitality, as against the sick-soul type, which is characterized by depressive isolation and dark divisions. These poles, as we saw, inform the Zoharic discussions and, in their wake, the teachings of the *Reshith Ḥokhmah*, wherein just this distinction structures the whole central discussion (*Shaʿar ha-ʾAhavah*, chap. 10). The energy of human joy, moreover, provides at the very least *the* mundane condition in classical rabbinic sources for divine indwelling, and for the invasion of the Holy Spirit of prophecy at best. This idea takes on strong theurgic qualities in the Jewish mystical mythology of joy, as we have seen, and it bears adding that Rabbi Ḥayim Vital in his great handbook on holiness and spiritual realization (*Shaʿarei Qedushah*) underscores sadness and joy in his discussion of the divine excess (*shefaʿ*) which may be induced to overflow into this world—healing the husks of negativity and illuminating its recipients with prophetic awareness (cf. 2.4; 3.4).

There is another aspect to the equation, and that is that the joyful service of God through the commandments transfigures the natural-ness of this-worldly actions. In his discussions of the phenomenon of conversion especially, William James also gave voice to this di-mesion—for the process of conversion, in his view, involves a convergence of "personal energy" toward a "religious center," such that one's "previous carnal self" is doubly transformed, both as a matter of self-awareness and in terms of potential performance. Indeed, as the wholly earthly self surrenders to a divine Source, the human will is typi-cally regenerated in and through emotional effusions that partake of transcendent reality. The gravity of the natural is lifted by a lightness of being that radiates grace. The so-called "divided self" which James also considers is, then, a person who not only swings between the poles of religious healthy-mindedness or sickness, but who bears the two in his conflicted soul—yearning for rebirth through a convergence of his parts towards one center, forever.

No Jewish saint exemplifies these psycho-spiritual matters as does Rabbi Naḥman of Bratzlav (1772–1810). Indeed, in him the raw ma-terials of the *Reshith Ḥokhmah* are distilled in a personal combustion of awesome tensions and demands. The embers of this inner fire still burn in innumerable teachings and tales. To begin, let us consider Rabbi Naḥman's retelling of the parable of his maternal great-grandfa-ther, Rabbi Israel Baʿal Shem, as retold and reinterpreted by the latter's grandson, Naḥman's uncle, Rabbi Moshe Ḥayim Ephraim of Sudilkov.

> Concerning joy (simḥah), (consider this) parable: Sometimes when people are rejoicing and dancing, they grab a man from outside (the circle)—one who is sad (be-ʿatzvut) and depressed—and press him against his will into the circle (maḥol) of dancers, and force him to rejoice with them. So it is with joy: for when a person is happy, his depression and sufferings stand off to the side. But the higher level is to struggle and pursue that very depression, and bring it also into the joy, until the depression is transformed into joy. . . . For (indeed:) there are (types of) sorrow and woe that are (manifestations of) the (demonic) Other Side, and do not want to be bearers of holiness; hence they flee from joy, and one must force them into (the sphere of) holiness—namely, joy—against their will, as (I) just said. (*Liqqutei Mo-haran, Tinyana'* 23)

This revision of the parable is remarkable. According to Rabbi Naḥman's reception, the social aspects of the earlier versions have been thoroughly psychologized. Indeed, the double circle of dancers is now the dramatic representation of a psychic division—an inner splitting, whereby the joyous celebrant temporarily cuts himself off from depressive deadness.[1] Significantly, Rabbi Naḥman affirms this momentary revitalization and does not reduce it to religious observance. That is not to deny or demote the joyful observance of the commandments. Innumerable teachings enforce their fundamental character. It is rather that Naḥman was also aware—and frequently noted—that religious joy may be regenerated from the most natural and seemingly frivolous of acts. Hence simple dance may have a catalytic catharsis, and lead toward a higher healing. But this requires the celebrant to direct the energies so elicited toward the divisive and depressive dimensions of the self—only partially and temporarily transcended by earthly joy. Accordingly, the master instructs his hearers to work for psychic wholeness. He urges a psychological activism which pursues the agents of one's depression in all their guises, and transforms them through the agency of joy.

Joy, then, is a divine dynamism which fuses the fragments of one's inner being, and transmutes demonic decay into holiness and health. As Rabbi Naḥman understands, the power of joy lies in its capacity for self-forgetting, in the momentary transcendence of naturalness. But a joy unredeemed, a joy which does not integrate inner demons into a higher wholeness, does not truly transform the person into a chariot of God's holiness. Therefore Naḥman goes on to say that it is a "great commandment" or "obligation" (*mitzvah gedolah*) to be "in joy always" (*be-simḥah tamid*), resisting the sickness (*hola'at*) of sadness with an ever-expanding joy (ibid., 24; also *Liqqutei ʿEtzot, simḥah,* 29–31). Then will the Shekhinah descend upon the sick (*holeh*) soul as a whirling sphere (*holah*) of dance (*maḥol* ["reworking"] *j. Sukkah, pereq lulav ve-ʿaravah; Num. Rab., Shemini* 11)—and heal its divisions. Rabbi Naḥman does not hesitate to call this a redemptive repair (*tiqqun*; cf. ibid., *Tinyana'* 24).

Now let us be clear: for a person like Rabbi Naḥman there is no question that, despite the nonhalakhic depiction of dancing in the parable, proper dancing always took place in the context of the commandments (*riqqudin shel mitzvah*)—as for example when one may be aroused to celebrate on festivals or weddings. In this regard, *riqqudin shel mitzvah* are no different from all other *mitzvot* whereby human praxis is sanctified through joyful devotion to God—and thus transcends the natural world. To the extent that there is a fall in religious consciousness, and the performance occurs perfunctorily or to satisfy egoistical or other urges (*behinat ha-yetzer*), then the offering is a "false fire" on the altar of divine service and strengthens the "forces of externality." The whole world is thus fraught with spiritual danger, and one may pass into transcendence only with utmost resoluteness.

True joy must therefore be strengthened and aroused; and for this Rabbi Nahman feels the need to offer counsels of a nonhalakhic order, repeating many of the dicta first offered by the *Reshith Hokhmah*— though now, of course, intensified or revised in accord with his own theological program. First among these *hanhagot* (or *regimen vitae*) is the practice of *hitboddedut*. This old meditative practice of physical and mental withdrawal was taken over by de Vidas as a means to generate joy. But while he retains the old techniques of mental fixation, Nahman introduces a strong verbal element. For a portion of every day, the seeker should withdraw to a place of sensory isolation and there open his heart to God in an uninhibited confession of his naturalness and distance from God. This deep broken-heartedness (*lev nishbar*; or what Rabbi Dov Ber called *tzubrochenhayt*) acts upon the soul by stilling the passions of the imagination and stimulating the roots of joy that link him—as by an inflamed charge—to God.

A complex circuit of energy is thus conceived, leading from troubled desire, through tears and talk before God, to a joy which heals the broken heart and stimulates wholehearted worship—and thence back to deeper moments of *hitboddedut*. The process is a purification of inwardness and development of a simplified service that overcomes intellection and ego. It is indeed a liberation (or *herut*), as Nahman says—though not from Nomos, which is its vehicle, but from Nature. A remarkable exegesis makes the point. Taking up the verse from Isa. 55:12, which predicts that the people "will leave (Babylon) in joy (*be-simhah*) and be led (homeward) secure (*be-shalom*)," the master teaches a personal path. If one works to leave one's inner exile of natural desire and confusion of thought *through* the joy of the Sabbath and other commandments, then a harmonious wholeness (*shelemut*) of mind will result—and with it true liberation. Countering the prophetic word, Rabbi Nahman converts the divine promise into a saintly condition: joy is now the spark of freedom, the first flame of a purified consciousness (*Liqqutei Moharan, Tinyana'* 17).

The highly privatized practice of *hitboddedut* is complemented by other, more interpersonal possibilities for the anomistic arousal of joy. These too conform to the sequence taught in the *Reshith Ḥokhmah*, but again with the unique Bratzlav twist. Thus where de Vidas stressed the value of seeing the face of a sage, Rabbi Naḥman naturally replaces this figure with the saint—through whom one may perceive the radiance of a higher joy shining through (*Liqqutei Moharan* 30.2). The result of this illumination is the stimulation of joy in the dormant spirit and the activation of energized service (*zerizut*) in the fulfillment of the commandments (*Liqqutei ʿEtzot, simḥah*, 1). The process of this return to inwardness by the Hasid is inaugurated by the process of journeying to one's spiritual master, or Tzaddiq, on Holy Days. This pilgrimage serves as an outward manifestation of the worshipper's progressive divestment of naturalness, and is complemented by acts of charity and gift-giving (*Liqqutei ʿEtzot, moʿadei ha-Shem*, 4–8). So prepared, the seeker may properly receive the radiant joy of the Tzaddiq's face through the eyes—whence they penetrate the inmost being and induce repentance (*Liqqutei ʿEtzot, ʿeynayim*, 1). The light of the saint's face thus opens up a space for introspection in the penitent. Revising the psalmist's cry "I will sing to the Lord as long as I live (*be-ʿodi*). . . . (Yea) I will rejoice (*'esmaḥ*) in the Lord" (Psalm 104:33–34), Rabbi Naḥman taught that one must begin one's song of spiritual renewal with whatever residue (*be-ʿodi*) of goodness can be found in the self—and devote that joyfully to God (see *Liqqutei Moharan* 1.282; *Liqqutei ʿEtzot, simḥah*, 29). With this rebirth of inner light, one may go into the world and rejuvenate the heart of each neighbor (*Liqqutei ʿEtzot, simḥah*, 28). Hereby the circuit of energy is a current of ethicized light.

The ideal of being "in joy always" (*be-simḥah tamid*) thus charges Rabbi Naḥman's thought with a certain messianic enlightenment. I mean this in the sense that the joyous service of God through the commandments turns the worshippers into purified prisms of divine light. And to the extent that this bond becomes an increasingly permanent attachment (*devequt*) to God, and is simultaneously extended across the social plane, the preternatural radiance of redemption penetrates and repairs the earthly realm. In this regard, the quest for holy simplicity (or *temimut*) in the service of God marks the realization that heavenly light can pass undiffused and unblocked only through a purified human vessel.

Some similar thoughts are already expressed by Naḥman's great ancestor, the holy Baʿal Shem. Not only does the terminology *tamid besimḥah* recur throughout the received corpus of this saint—and often, too, as an antidote to sadness—but we also have a citation in which the Baʿal Shem reportedly emphasized how the joyfulness of simple human piety can stimulate joy in the highest realms. Nevertheless, I believe that these influences ultimately derive from de Vidas' *Reshith Ḥokhmah*, and that it is this work in particular that explains the structure of Naḥman's metaphysics of joy. I have initiated my case earlier. At this juncture we must merely recall that for de Vidas joy is the soul of faith and the bond of attachment which connects the heavenly and human realms in a current of preternatural light. Indeed, by the joyous performance of the commandments both the worshipper on earth and the Shekhinah in heaven are restored to a redemptive wholeness—which brings me back to dancing.

Rabbi Naḥman's emphasis on dance, as we have reported it so far, has a particularly psycho-spiritual dimension. That point is fully underscored by the homily concerning the descent of the Shekhinah to heal the worshipper like some cosmic ringmaster. And so we must be grateful to the larger concordance of thought between de Vidas and Naḥman to turn our attention to what might otherwise be lost: the mystical mythology of joy in Bratzlav theology. To bring this into view, let us first recall the remarkable Zoharic reinterpretation of Psalm 148 (*Piqqudei* 2.232b) reproduced in the *Reshith Ḥokhmah* (*Shaʿar ha-'Ahavah* 10.8-12). Hereby, the whole heavenly host is envisaged as a Cosmic Anthropos; and more specifically, the "angelic messengers" (*mal'akhav*) of the psalm represent "the two Pillars which exist under the Body" (*trein qayamin de-gayemu teḥot gufa'*)—namely, the sefirotic gradations known as *netzaḥ* (Eternity) and *hod* (Splendor), which function as the Feet of the *Corpus Mysticum*. The recitation of this psalm with mystical intent may thus mystically activate, strengthen, or otherwise repair these pillars of the cosmic structure as a whole (cf. 10.18).

Rabbi Naḥman's teaching is more allusively wrought. In one passage he no more than remarks, in the most general way, that dances performed joyously for the service of God (*riqqudin shel mitzvah*) combat the demonic powers (the *ḥitzonim* and *dinim*)—since the irradiation of joy to the dancing feet "banishes" their "hold" or "constraint" (*Liqqutei 'Etzot, simḥah*, 12). At first glance, there seems to be nothing special here—perhaps no more than a spiritual therapeutics of sorts. What makes our eyes widen is the repetition of these comments *along with* the comment that "feet" represent *netzaḥ* and *hod*—the heavenly gradations also known symbolically as Prophets. This allows the master to invoke Psalm 90:12 ("Teach us to number our days, that *we may obtain a wise heart, [ve-navi' levav ḥokhmah]*)," and transform it mythically. The phrase is now taken to describe a theurgic possibility whereby heartfelt (*levav*) joy may elevate the feet to transcendent heights. In more cosmic terms, this means that the cycle of energy activated through dance may simultaneously redeem "all the lower realms which are (symbolically) called 'feet'"—both those on earth and in heaven (*Liqqutei Moharan, Tinyana'* 81). In the case of dancing before the bride, the elevation of feet is actually said to induce healing elements to flow from the Supernal Mother (*binah; levav*) to her virgin daughter below (specifically, her share in the Holy Name; see *Liqqutei Moharan* 1.32). So sweetened, she will ascend her conjugal bed in joy—and reciprocally activate Holy Unions in the Highest Realms.

Dance is thus conceived here as a mystery rite—and something approaching pure religious form, which resembles nothing so much as a ray of simple and infinitely expanding light. For Rabbi Naḥman of Bratzlav the spark of this illumination is joy, and it projects the hidden path to God. All one's longing must therefore be for this birth of joy in the soul and its sacrificial devotion to God. In a poignant prayer, Naḥman articulates the passion of this desire—and with it I shall end.

> Truly You know, O Lord, our God, that we are (but) flesh and blood, and our thoughts are very mixed and confounded with various types of foolishness and madness—to the extent that they ambush us with foolish thoughts of distraction and pride . . . (and) I can hardly open my mouth and say anything to You in a straight-forward, truthful and proper manner. What can I do? Where might I flee or turn, and from where will my help come in my great sorrow? Even when I cry out and groan in prayer, what can I say to find favor—since I am overwhelmed to distraction by all these thoughts and confusions? Surely (You) God have found my (very) sin—so do with me what You will, I am in Your hands like clay. (But just) have mercy, mercy! Just save and rescue (me . . .) from death to life, from sorrow to joy, and from gloom to great light. Have mercy upon me (God), in Your great mercy, that the

merit and power of the true *tzaddiqs* will protect me, and that I may merit through them to utterly break the grip of pride, and perceive in absolute truthfulness my lowliness in every limb and fibre of my being. Then will my heart and mind be absent of all pride and haughtiness, and I shall merit the truest humility and most perfect faith. . . . And help me (O God) to bind myself in truth to the holy spirit of the true *tzaddiqs*, that I might thereby infuse into my being their holy spirit and be upright with (You) always in truth and perfect faith and truest humility. And then will I merit, through Your mercy, that this holy spirit be drawn into my arms and legs, until I may merit "to repair the defect of the arms and legs" (Above and Below); and to reveal and light up the illumination of the arms and legs—that my mind be aroused to great joy for Your great and true Name, until this holy joy trans-fuse my arms and legs, and that I clap in holy dance in such a manner that we may sweeten the (demonic) judgments from us and all Your people Israel. . . . And may I further merit, through Your mercy, to lift, raise up, and elevate my hands and feet and purify them from every defect. O Master of the Universe! Strengthen weakened hands and stumbling legs! Have mercy upon me, and purify and sanctify my hands and feet. . . . Deliver my feet from bondage and death, that through Your mercy they might be delivered unto life . . . ; and as for my hands, so stained and defective through impure acts, deliver them to purity. Be compassionate and forgiving unto me, through Your great mercy, for all ruptures and defects my hands and legs have caused; and grant that now and forever my limbs will be pure and sanctified for Your service—so that I may merit to raise my hands and feet to their holy Source (Above), that their great light be revealed, and I may clap and dance in and through this holiness. (*Liqqutei Tefillot* 10, *ad fin.*, pp. 28–29)

NOTES

1. For a related understanding, see A. Green, *Tormented Master: The Life and Spiritual Quest of Rabbi Naḥman of Bratzlav* (Tuscaloosa: University of Alabama Press, 1979), pp. 141f.

The Buddha's Smile:
Enlightenment and the Pursuit of Happiness
ROBERT A. F. THURMAN

PREAMBLE

THE DECLARATION OF INDEPENDENCE states that we all have rights to "life, liberty, and the pursuit of happiness." But what is this "happiness" that we are pursuing? Is there only one kind? There are physical and mental happiness, both of which seem to alternate with pain. There is the happiness of relief from pain. Is there a happiness that goes beyond the mere absence of pain and reaches what we might call bliss or beatitude? "Hedonism" is said to be the pursuit of sense pleasure, and has tended to be frowned upon by philosophers East and West. But is there anything wrong with the pursuit of bliss in heaven by Dante, the bliss of union with Christ by Theresa de Avila, the pursuit of the bliss of enlightenment by a bodhisattva? The Buddhist position is hard to discern clearly on this all-important issue—perhaps there are many different positions in the different regions of Buddhist thought and history. But as we examine the record, a clear picture begins to emerge.

Lately I have been reflecting about a salient fact of Buddhist history or myth. Siddhartha supposedly became a Buddha, a perfectly enlightened being, at the moment of greeting the morning star in the pre-dawn twilight under the Bodhi tree on a full-moon May morning in some year round-about 528 BCE. To become perfectly enlightened is not just to slip into some disconnected euphoria, an oceanic feeling of mystic oneness apart from ordinary reality. It is not to be invested by some God with the final word, a message to believe in and to promulgate. It is not even to come up with a solution, a sort of formula that can control reality. Rather it is supposed to be an experience of release from all compulsions and sufferings, combined with a precise awareness of any relevant object of knowledge; both of which naturally issue in a powerful sense of unbounded connectedness with the conditions of other beings, which gives limitless energy to an infinite love that wants those beings to become happier. A Buddha should know everything that matters and the precise nature of it all—that is how he or she is defined.

THESIS IN A NUTSHELL

The story goes that, upon attaining his perfect realization, the Buddha smiled! Fortunately for all concerned! The point is he could have frowned. Or he could have remained passive and inert. Or he could have beamed away like a Star Trek officer, turned into little sparkles—then to be no more. But the Buddha of our story smiled a cheerful smile.

"Buddha" is the designation for a person who comes to the peak of sentient evolution, beyond the stages and states of humans and even Gods. It is defined as "awakened" from the sleep of misknowledge, and "blossomed" into the omniscience and competence of universal compassion.[1] This stage of being has many other names: *Bhagavān* ("beautiful" or "glorious");[2] *Tathāgata* ("transcendingly realized") and, most important in our context, *Sugata* ("blissful"; *sukham-gata*, "having become bliss"). Such a being is described as having three bodies, bodies of Truth, Beatitude, and Emanation. In any sort of Buddhism, it seems beyond question that "Buddhahood" is a synonym for supreme happiness. To state my thesis succinctly, from the Buddhist perspective, enlightenment is happiness. So naturally a Buddha smiles.

In the Individual, Monastic, or "Early Buddhist" Vehicle,[3] Buddha is called Sugata, Blissful One. He is said to have attained both Nirvana and Parinirvana, all suffering "blown out" and "utterly blown out," to have reached the supreme happiness (*paramasukha*), to have gone beyond the Gods in joy, to have become the God of the Gods. In the Universal, Messianic, or Social Buddhist Vehicle, Buddhas are said to enjoy a Beatific Body (*Sambhogakāya*), to experience nonduality of Nirvana and the world, and are depicted as theistically capable of producing whole universes of bliss, buddhaverses (*buddhakshetra*) of Bliss

(*Sukhavati*), Intense Delight (*Abhirati*) and so forth. And in the Light-
ning, Diamond, or Apocalyptic Vehicle, ultimate reality as experienced
in enlightenment is described as bliss-void indivisible (*sukhashunyā-
vibhaga*). So the overall Buddhist view must be that supreme enlightenment and true happiness are one and the same.

Further, there seems to be a claim, implicit or explicit, that true
happiness is what all beings really want, and that all their pursuits of
even negative, unsatisfying, illicit, long-term destructive, addictive
forms of happiness are ineffective, erroneously guided attempts to
gain the true happiness of Nirvana. Shantideva makes this clear in his
Guide to the Bodhisattva Career:

> First of all I should make an effort to meditate upon the equality
> of self and others: I should protect all beings as I do myself, be-
> cause we are all equal in wanting happiness and not wanting
> suffering. Likewise all the different sentient beings in their pleas-
> ure and their pain, have a wish to be happy that is the same as
> mine. . . . (8.90–91)[4]

Here we see a major Buddhist claim, that all beings are equal in
that all are naturally concerned with the pursuit of happiness. This
appears to be assumed as self-evident. "Will not the ocean of joy that
shall exist when all beings are free be sufficient for me? What am I
doing wishing for my liberation alone?" (Shantideva, *Guide*, 8.108).

Here the attainment of Buddhahood, the social experience of
enlightenment wherein the world becomes a buddhaverse and all
beings' freedom goes along with the individual's freedom, is described
as an "ocean of joy."

And finally, "129. Whatever joy there is in this world, all comes
from desiring others to be happy, and whatever suffering there is in
this world, all comes from desiring myself to be happy. 130. What
need is there to say much more? The childish work for their own
benefit. The Buddhas work for the benefit of others. Just look at the
difference between them."

Here, the cause of this happiness of Buddhahood is argued to be
the spirit of enlightenment of love and compassion (*maitrī-karuna-
bodhi-chitta*), the altruistic concern for the happiness of others. This
selfless will for others' happiness is further claimed to underlie all happinesses, all joys, even "normal" ones, that are dismissed in the first
Holy Fact as the "suffering of change."

How can we say that all joy comes from the altruistic will? Some objectors will argue for aesthetic experience, where the connoisseur seeks sheer pleasure in music, painting, food, and so on, quite ignorant of others' happiness. Others talk of the joy in beating another in competition. And the most daring talk of sexual joy, where they can find plenty of pleasure just fulfilling their own desires without concern for the other's pleasure. Shantideva's commentaries are laconic in their arguments supporting this claim of his. So the general answer I have developed is twofold. First, the background answer is that the very human body with its great sensitivity which enables the hedonist or aesthete to enjoy great pleasures is the product of justice, the interactive virtue of moral behavior on the part of the person who has worked through less sensitive life forms to become a human. Second, the more immediate answer is that the essence of the pleasure the aesthete gets comes from his or her diminishing of self-concern and attachment. In a good meal, the pleasure lies in forgetting the self in the joy of overcoming hunger. In music one forgets the self and floats away on the heavenly sounds. In encountering a great work of art, one is lifted out of the habitual perimeter of self-obsession into a moment of freer sensibility. And in sexual experience, there is a large literature which claims that unsatisfying sex is sex dominated by self-enclosure and self-preoccupation, and that the sensitivity and joy expand immeasurably with concern for the partner and the overcoming of self-consciousness. So the joy Shantideva talks about is precisely proportional to the degree of replacement of self-preoccupation by other-preoccupation, self-cherishing by other-cherishing.

But if it is so that enlightenment is true happiness, and the Buddha taught his Dharma considering humans widely capable of attaining it, then why is Buddhism considered a pessimistic, nihilistic, even morbid religion or philosophy? And this not only by moderns in the West, but by some Brahmins at various times in India, some Mandarins at various times in China, and other authorities all over countries where Buddhism flourished for millennia?

I think the essence of the answer lies in the corollary of the thesis "enlightenment is happiness"; namely, that "ignorance is misery." Compared to the joyous bliss of freedom and released awareness, the Buddha saw the plight of beings in bondage and confusion as an unremitting condition of suffering. Hence, in the diagnosis that he submitted to the world, the first Noble Truth (or "Holy Fact," as I prefer) was that all misknowledge-driven living is constant misery.

The *Dhammacakka-pavattana Sutta*[5] records him as saying simply, "All *this* is misery," the commentarial tradition informing us that the "this" refers to the "contaminated aggregates" (*sāsravaskandha*) of the misknowing body-mind complex.

So it must have easily seemed to people who felt happy now and then that the Buddha was profoundly pessimistic. They tended to fasten on the first Holy Fact of Suffering as proof of a grim outlook. It was not clear to them that the reason he called this the first "Holy Fact" was that he was aware that it was a "fact" only for a "holy" person, a person who has seen the lack of intrinsically real self. Ordinary egocentric individuals consider the universality of suffering an erroneous judgement, not a fact or a truth. Ordinary egocentric life alternates between pain and pleasure, suffering and happiness. Buddha understood that alternation, and called ordinary happiness "suffering of change," because of its instability. He did so not because he wanted to deny what little happiness people do find, but because he wanted them to discover for themselves an infinitely higher order of happiness, what might be called true happiness. So the Buddha vs. the normal world on happiness boils down to the two conflicting positions: "Relative happiness is all the happiness there is and it's good enough for us," vs. "Relative happiness is just punctuation in the rhythm of suffering; but fortunately there is an absolute happiness that is greater, deeper, secure, and ultimately blissful."

Well, then, who's right and who wrong? Is it merely a matter of opinion? It would be a matter of opinion if the perceptions of the two types of beings, egocentric beings and Buddhas, were equal. But a Buddha is supposed to have a superior perception, to see through illusion and discern reality. So an egocentric person who considered a Buddha to be another type of egocentric person would certainly argue that it was his word against the Buddha's. But the Buddha argued that it is fact and not opinion. It is a fact that all this is suffering for an unenlightened person, and that this fact is only known by an enlightened person. The unenlightened are like Plato's cave-dwellers. Only the one who has escaped and seen the sun knows that they are trapped in the shadows. To think this through for ourselves, we have to understand how the Buddha analyzed the ordinary person's misperception, to see if the analysis makes sense.

The cause of the symptom of universal suffering, according to Buddha, is ignorance (*avidya*). This ignorance is not merely a passive failure to know some things. It is an active misknowing of everything.

It is a knowing of things to be what they are not in reality (*a-sad-vidya*). I prefer to call it a misknowledge. Most basically, the ordinary being knows that she is herself, she is there. Her presence is an irreducible reality, fixed, unique, constant, and independent. Each of us feels that way. In fact if we for a moment lost track of who or what we were, if we could not recognize ourselves, we would consider that a sign of sickness and seek medical help. Similarly, we each see things as having fixed essences that correspond to our notions of them, serving as the referents of the names we give them. We know we have a fixed identity and things have fixed identities, and these identities are intrinsic, objective, identifiable, and irreducible.

But there are certain problems deriving from this knowledge we have. The first is that while we are sure of self, "other" becomes problematic. Cognitively it is problematic because, like Descartes, we may always doubt that the other, the rest of the universe, is actually there. It could be simply an elaborate illusion. We can only be sure of ourselves, our constant being, the receiving point of our perceptions and the source of our thoughts. Emotionally it is problematic because the other is so much greater than the self. It is infinite and eternal, and it goes beyond our limits of space and time. Our perception gets lost in it. We die in it. And other beings, we dimly realize, have a perception opposite to ours. They think they are the absolute center of the universe, even though we know we are. So we are pitted against them, they against us. Thus we feel insecure and anxious; we desire things in order to expand our sphere of security. We hate others for expanding their spheres of security. We fear they will do to us what we want to do to them. We are proud when we feel momentarily on top. We are envious when they seem above us for the moment.

Thus our basic knowledge of our presence, reality, and identity reveals to us a predicament that is naturally unpleasant. Here we are, concrete and self-evidently undeniable, up against all others, outnumbered and basically waiting to lose whatever it is. It is Hobbes' "war of all against all." We live in constant dissatisfaction. We live in fear and trembling, feeling essentially unique and alone, isolated and alienated from all others and the cosmos itself. This knowledge places our very heart in a kind of vice, a perpetual state of being squeezed by the usually subliminal awareness of the untenability of our situation. Naturally, as with any chronic pain, we get used to it. We get so we hardly notice it, and we measure our days by our little escapes and successes, by the momentary pleasures we experience from any slight relief or distraction from our basic condition, that is, being pitted against an unrelenting, consuming, and infinite alien universe. And in a world of other beings suffering under the same core constriction of innermost being, we develop a mutual agreement not to draw attention to our shared chronic stress of alienation, but to reinforce each other in making do.

What the Buddha discovered was that our knowledge of our distinct, individual, irreducible identity is actually a misknowledge. The crushing vice gripping our heart is simply the result of an error. If the seemingly absolute self were mobilized to focus all its powers on the verification of its own existence, it could only come up with an eventually definitive failure to discover itself. No atomic self, no individual could be found to resist analysis by the ultimate-reality-seeking analytic cognition. When the Buddha experienced this definitive failure to discover an intrinsic identity in the self, any real thing to correspond to the habitual sense of the absolute self, he experienced a total meltdown of his own personal heart-vice. The vice squeezed itself to the limit, as it were, and found itself squeezing against itself, with nothing sensitive in the middle, with nothing to hold on to. As with a pair of pliers with nothing in the grippers, infinite pressure could do no good, could do no damage. When he experienced this space-like equi-poised *samadhi*—the direct experience of selflessness or voidness—he felt an overwhelming relief. He felt free of fear from any other, totally free on the level of his accustomed absolute intrinsic identity. And yet he was also free of any reified state of isolated freedom, and so relatively totally interconnected with the whole world. He felt no more loneliness and alienation; he was no longer pitted against the world but a part of the world, a part of other beings and they a part of him. There was no opponent for him; he no longer lacked anything. What a monumental relief! As if an iron vice-grip that had been squeezing on the heart were suddenly removed; this is the happiness of enlightenment. No wonder every ordinary happiness, pleasure of sense experience, or mental pleasure seemed paltry and insignificant next to the basic condition of the misknowing, a condition of being squeezed internally by the steel trap of the identity habit.

In the Individual Vehicle, the happiness of Nirvana, or spiritual release, tends to be stated only in negative terms, as the cessation of suffering, freedom from bondage, the final accomplishment, the laying down of the burden, and so on. The Buddha refuses to discuss whether a Realized Lord exists after death, does not, both does and does not, neither does nor does not. Sometimes we hear of the "city of Nirvana," the "gates of Nirvana," the "isle of Nirvana," the "other shore of Nirvana." And very occasionally it is referred to as "peace," "bliss," "clear light," and so on.

The third Holy Fact or Noble Truth is the one that Buddha staked his life's work on, the Holy Fact of Cessation of Suffering. This was his good news, his discovery that he found worth sharing with other beings. Upon realizing his own freedom, he is reported to have said, "Deep, peaceful, fabrication-free, translucent, uncreated—I have discovered a Reality like elixir of immortality. Whoever I might teach about it, they won't understand; better to stay in silence in the forest!"[6] Later, when he had become more optimistic about people's ability to respond to his instructions, he sent out his mendicants to spread the word, telling them to announce that "The gates of Nirvana have been opened!"

The words for happiness and joy, *sukha, ānanda, muditā, saumanasya, prīti*, and so on, tend to be used in more relativistic contexts. For example, the first *dhyāna* ("contemplative realm") contains intense happiness and rapture (*sukha* and *prīti*), and the later realms go into an equanimity that is beyond such pleasure. There is a state beyond the fourth formless trance (*ārūpyasamāpatti*) called the cessation of sensation and thought, although in the *Parinibbānasutta*, for example, the Buddha emerges from that cessation, moves back down through the trances and contemplation, and attains Parinibbana from the fourth-form realm contemplation.[7]

In sum, in the Individual Vehicle, it seems that the Buddha feels great compunction not to stress the positive image of Nirvana, and to equate liberation with something as much beyond pleasure or happiness as it is beyond pain or suffering. We have to decide whether this means that the Buddha and his early followers actually thought of enlightenment as oblivion, and would not have equated it with happiness. Obviously, my thesis is that this is an incorrect interpretation. The evidence for my thesis is the fact that, granting his restraint in talking of a positive state of Nirvana, he explicitly denies that Nirvana is a state of oblivion, explicitly differentiating it from the realm of absolute nothingness (*akimānyayatana*), the realm beyond consciousness and unconsciousness (*naivāsamjñā-naivāsamjñāyātana*), and even the realm of cessation of thought and sensation (*cittavedanānirodha*).

In the Universal Vehicle, there is no hesitancy in describing the realm of enlightenment in the most glowing terms, especially as the tradition develops. In the Universal Vehicle Scriptures, there is frequent mention of the happiness of Buddhahood, social and cosmic, the perfecting and adorning of the buddhaverse, and the liberating of all beings. A Buddha is described as having a "Beatific Body" (*samhhogakāya*), indicating that a Buddha's experience of combining oneness with ultimate reality is a changeless condition of intense delight and joy. In such ways, in the Universal Vehicle, happiness is brought to the fore and explicated as necessary for the overcoming of suffering.

There is a parable in the *Mahāyāna Parinirvāna Sūtra*,[8] wherein Shariputra complains to Buddha that, if the nature of enlightenment was pure bliss, goodness, eternal peace, and so forth, how come he hadn't told the Disciples, but had taught them about impermanence, suffering, selflessness, and impurity? The Buddha responds with an elaborate parable about a nursing mother whose infant is deadly ill. A skilled physician comes to her and gives her medicine that will save her baby, but cautions her that, while the medicine is working, she must not give the baby any of her mother's milk. When she protests that that would be too difficult, since the baby will cry and demand the milk, he gives her a foul-tasting ointment to rub on her nipples. She smeared it on and when the baby tried to drink, the foulness made it not want the nipple after all. After the illness had been cured, she then washed her nipples and invited her boy to drink again. But it took some coaxing before the suspicious boy would drink. In this parable, the Buddha's *Lotus-Sutra*-style teaching of the goodness, purity, changeless bliss, and freedom of the buddhaverse is likened to his mother's milk. The medicine is the underlying presence of this teaching hidden within the Individual Vehicle. And the grim emphasis on the truth of suffering, the meditations of impurity, selflessness, emptiness, and so forth, are the foul-tasting ointment.

In the beginning of the *Flower Ornament Sutra*, the Buddha is depicted just at the moment of his realization of perfect enlightenment.[9] His state is clearly not just a "spiritual," "other-worldly," contentless awareness of a heavenly expanse, or a blank infinity, or a realm of nothingness, an extinct oblivion. Being an emanation of a Body of Reality and a Body of Beatitude, his enlightenment involves the reconnection of his awareness with all reality, not only in its ultimate freedom from intrinsic identity but also in its network of specific inter-connections.

This is powerfully confirmed on the imaginal level by the trans-formation of the environment that expresses this enlightenment. Within the energization of the Buddha's explosion of awareness, the land, the trees, the architecture of the environment are transformed from gross, fixed, substantial earth, water, fire, and air, into jewel-like energies of concentrated glory in a rich realm of beauty. These em-bodiments of wisdom and love manifest the color, life-energy, positive mental energies of bodhisattvas and enlightening beings. This trans-formation shows that enlightenment is attained by self and environ-ment interdependently. The environment expresses its attainment by displaying its miraculousness.

The scene shows that seemingly inert atoms are filled with life forms. The enlightenment "tree emanated light; within the light there rained precious stones, and within each gem there were enlightening beings, in great hosts like clouds. . . ."[10] Within atoms there were micro-universes, from which millions of enlightening bodhisattvas emerged, coming to this site and dimension to celebrate the Buddha's manifestation of the attainment of enlightenment. Thus the ordinary, seemingly inert, one-dimensional, inorganic universe is revealed as alive, as overflowing with loving beings.

In spite of the greater degree of explicitness of the teaching of universal happiness of the buddhaverse, the Universal Vehicle still pre-sents the ultimate nonduality in terms of the indivisibility of wisdom and compassion. Compassion (*karuṇā*), though itself the most positive emotion, is oriented toward the negative reality of suffering. Thus compassion is defined as the will to relieve others of their sufferings. Love (*maitrī*), on the other hand, is defined as the will to connect beings to happiness. A bodhisattva could not connect any beings to happiness if there was no happiness to be found anywhere. Only if the bodhisattva has discovered a well of happiness within him- or herself is it possible to actualize the good will that is called love.

Thus, as the Universal Vehicle develops, its initial procedure of emphasizing compassion to neutralize others' sufferings begins to give way to the more positive activity of actually sending happiness to others, developing an energy source within wisdom of liberated bliss in order to transmit to others something more than just the possibility of dulling their sufferings. This is vividly depicted in numerous Uni-versal Vehicle Sutras.

However, just how this is done technically is not fully explicated in the exoteric Universal Vehicle. In the esoteric Diamond, Thunderbolt (Vajra), or Process (Tantra) Vehicle, which I call the "Apocalyptic Vehicle," wisdom and compassion are replaced by wisdom and *bliss*. Here the "art" (*upāya*) of Buddhahood depends on the energy of great bliss (*mahāsukha*). This nonduality of bliss and void is the happiness of Vajradharahood, spiritual, social, cosmic, and aesthetic, sensuous, and even sexual. It is the bliss-void indivisibility of cosmic orgasm, symbolized in the Father-Mother-Union embodiments of the supreme experience of enlightenment, the male Vajradhara as orgasmic bliss-wisdom (*sahajānanda-jñāna*) in union with the Universal Mother, Void-form-nondual (*Vishvamātā-shūnyarūpa*) Transcendent Wisdom (*Prajñāpāramitā*), the Universal Consort (*Mahāmudrā*), the Great Perfection (*Mahāsandhi*) of consummate union with the All-good Mother Goddess Transcendent Wisdom, and so forth. Here the technicalities of the art of embodying enlightenment are set forth in intricate detail. The architecture of the buddhaverse and the subtle neurology of the Buddha body are taught to the practitioner, harnessing the visualizing powers of the imagination and the artistic creativity of the subtle mind, normally only released into activity at the times of dreaming, death, or orgasmic melting. Here we can recall Saraha's "Enlightenment Verses" (*doha*):

13. Whoever deprived of the orgasmic (bliss), seeks Nirvana, Can in no wise acquire the absolute truth. . . .[11]

Here I translate the Sanskrit *sahaja* (which Snellgrove translates "the Innate") as "orgasmic." This choice is crucial for our understanding of the essence of Tantric Buddhism. *Sahaja* literally means "born together"; hence "innate" is not wrong. It is opposed to *parikalpita*, "mentally constructed," when used adjectivally to modify terms for mental functions, such as misknowledge. However, the *sahaja* Saraha here intends is not just the "instinctual" or "innate." It stands for *sahaja-ānanda*, the orgasmic bliss that is experienced when the gross sense of self melts, when the neural energies and neuro-substances have melted and fused into the central channel of the subtle yogic nervous system. When this fusion moves from the brain center to the throat center, it is called "bliss"; when from the throat to the heart it is called "supreme bliss"; when from the heart to the navel it is "distinctive bliss"; and when it culminates by moving from the navel center to the genital center, it is called *sahajānanda*, which I have translated "orgasmic bliss." It is not the conventional orgasm resulting in the spasms of seminal or vaginal emission. But it is a sustained dissolving of self at the subtlest level, moving far beyond the orgasm of normal sexuality. It is a much more intense melting and bliss suffusion. Its worldly metaphor, however, is the human orgasm, just as the metaphor of the union of absolute and relative, the Tantric explication of Buddhahood, is the sexual union of male and female, the Father-Mother-Union we see so often represented in Tantric art. Therefore, the Tantric explication of enlightenment is that it is a kind of cosmic orgasm, beyond sexuality but departing from its greatest intensity, the integration of all polarities in the boundless life and bliss of Buddhahood. If we can even imagine this, then Tantras will have given us the feeling, "Ah! So that's why he is smiling!" Certainly Saraha's vision is that this "fourth state of bliss" is what the whole world's frantic activity is all about. This is the treasure, the bliss, the fruition all beings are drawn to like moths to the flame. He goes on to reject all ordinary definitions of goal and practices:

> 16. Abandon such false attachments! Renounce such illusions! / Than knowledge of This (the orgasmic) there is nothing else. / Other than This no one can know.
> 17. It is This that's read and This that's meditated, / It's This that's discussed in treatises and old legends. / There's no school of thought that doesn't have This as its aim, / But one only sees it at the foot of one's master.
> 18. If the word of one's master but enter the heart, / It seems like a treasure in the palm of one's hand. / The world is enslaved by falsehood, Says Saraha, / And the fool does not perceive his true nature.
> 19. Without meditating, without renouncing the world, / One may stay at home in the company of one's wife. / Can that be called perfect knowledge, Saraha says, / If one is not released while enjoying the pleasures of sense?
> 20. By that same essence by which one is born, lives, and dies, By means of that one gains the highest bliss.
> But though Saraha speaks these deep and mysterious words, This stupid world seems not to understand. . . .
> 26. Do not discriminate but see things as one, / Making no distinction of families. / Let the whole of the three realms / Become one in the state of great passion.

The "great passion" here is far beyond the usual lust for sexual objectives, in that it is the urge to merge with all others, to transcend the rigidities of the boundaries of the self and open to identify with all life, to feel the feelings of all beings, to share one's innermost joy with all living things. This universal passion (*mahārāga, sarvānurāgana*) is the ultimate expression of universal compassion transforming to universal love, energized by inexhaustible bliss.

27. Here there is no beginning, middle or end, / Neither the life-cycle nor nirvana. / In this state of highest bliss, / There is neither self nor other.

Of course there is always the possibility that the integration of the three vehicles, Monastic, Messianic, and Apocalyptic, is a Tibetan invention, and the real situation in India was much more diverse, with the later vehicles actually emerging in opposition to one another, and people calling themselves Buddhist actually up to opposite tasks, leading to different goals. Some make this argument, and they may be right. But I do not read the record in this way. My main reason for not doing so is that India has always been the world's easiest place in which to start a religion. If the new Messianic and Apocalyptic movements called Mahayana and Vajrayana were opposed to Monastic Buddhism and to each other, the leaders of either one could have simply attached it to a couple of imposing *Upanishads*, cooked up a *Purāṇa* or two, and proclaimed the new revelation as coming straight from Vishnu, Shiva, or the Mother Goddess. How much more convenient it would have been for them if they wanted to "imitate Hinduism" simply to be Hindus! Always room for more saints and sages in India. Therefore, if they attached themselves to Buddhism, they must have understood themselves as Buddhists, and so must have considered themselves as unpacking the inner intentions of the Buddha in their own particular eras in response to new circumstances in the land and new insights of their own.

So, if there is one thing that links them all together, it is that all consider themselves useful vehicles for beings to ride upon in their beginningless and endless pursuit of, and even attainment of, sheer happiness.

In conclusion, let me quote at length from the *Ashokāvadāna*'s page-long, stock description of the Buddha's smile:

Then, the Beautiful Lord smiled. It is the rule that when the Beautiful Buddhas smile, then blue, yellow, red, and white rays and rays which are of the color of madder, crystal, and silver issue forth from their mouths. Some go upwards and some go downwards. Those which go downwards go to the hells named Revival, Black-Line, Crushing, Screaming, Great Screaming, Burning, Intense Burning, Unremitting, Blister, Extreme Blister, Shattering, Shivering, Shuddering, Blossom, Lotus, and Great Lotus. Becoming cold they descend into the eight hot hells ending with Unremitting, and becoming hot they descend into the eight cold hells. . . .

The rays which go upwards go to the Four-Great-King-Heaven (and others), where they proclaim loudly, "Impermanence, suffering, emptiness, and absence of self." And they recite two stanzas, "Bestir yourselves. Go forth from the worldly life. Apply yourselves to the teachings of the Buddha. Destroy the army of death as an elephant destroys a hut of reeds. He who will walk without heedlessness in this Truth and its Discipline will free himself from rebirth, and will make an end of suffering."

Then these rays, after they have traversed this great universe, go following along close behind the Beautiful One. If the Beautiful One desires to predict the future they disappear in his breast. If he desires to predict a rebirth in hell they disappear in the sole of his foot. If he desires to predict a rebirth as an animal they disappear in his ankle. If he desires to predict a rebirth as a *preta* they disappear in his big toe. If he desires to predict a rebirth as a man they disappear in his knee. If he desires to predict the kingdom of a minor world monarch they disappear in the palm of his left hand. If he desires to predict the kingdom of a world emperor they disappear in the palm of his right hand. If he desires to predict a rebirth as a god they disappear in his navel. If he desires to predict the enlightenment of a layman they disappear in his mouth. If he desires to predict the enlightenment of a Love Buddha they disappear in his *ūrṇa*. If he desires to predict a supreme and perfect enlightenment they disappear in his *uṣhṇiṣha*.[12]

Perhaps this is the place to end this paper, with the light-rays disappearing into the Buddha's *uṣhṇiṣha*, as he prepares to predict all beings' unexcelled perfect enlightenment, their pursuit and actual enjoyment of the highest happiness.

NOTES

1. This definition of *Buddha* as *vibuddha* and *prabuddha* occurs in Yaśomitra, *Abhidharmakośavyākhyā*, chap. 1, p. 1.

2. *Bhagavān* is often translated "Blessed One," which emerges from the theistic Christian tradition that a holy person must be blessed by a higher being, or "Exalted One," which has a rather "Oriental" sense of honor attached to it. The Tibetan translation is elaborate, using the three consonants as three verb roots. More simply, *bhaga* means "glory," "fortune," even "beauty," so I think "glorious" or "beauteous" a more cheerful translation.

3. My terms for the Vehicles are idiosyncratic, so I will list them in table form.

    Hinayana - Individual or Monastic Vehicle
    Mahayana - Universal or Messianic Vehicle
    Vajrayana - Diamond or Apocalyptic Vehicle

4. Shantideva, *Guide to the Bodhisattva Career*, trans. S. Batchelor (Dharamsala: LTWA, 1984).

5. See M. Walshe, *Thus Have I Heard* (Boston: Wisdom, 1992).

6. This verse is common in Tibetan accounts of the Buddha life, most probably from the *Lalitavīstara Sūtra*.

7. Walshe, *Thus Have I Heard.*

8. This parable was read to me during a class on Buddhist Chinese from the Chinese text, by Dr. Thomas Cleary, in 1988. There is not yet an English translation available.

9. Thomas Cleary, trans., *The Flower Ornament Sutra* (Boston: Shambhala, 1993).

10. Ibid.

11. Basic translation by D. Snellgrove (altered by me to accord with my terminology), printed in E. Conze et al., *Buddhist Texts Through the Ages* (New York: Harper, 1954).

12. This passage is adapted, with altered terminology, from W. E. Clark's unpublished manuscript of the *Dīvyāvadāna*.

Happiness in the Confucian Way

TU WEI-MING

THERE IS SOMETHING ETHICALLY elevating about Jesus Christ's exhortation to turn the other cheek: it appeals to the streak of self-effacing idealism in many of us. We believe that this unilateral altruism symbolizes a higher virtue than simply the revengeful "eye for an eye and tooth for a tooth." It might come as a surprise that another response is possible, no less noble, but characterized by lofty pragmatism rather than sheer idealism. When Confucius was asked: "Should one not return malice with kindness?" he replied, "If you return malice with kindness, what will you return kindness with? Therefore, return malice with uprightness (justice), but return kindness with kindness."[1] Perhaps, for us, the more intriguing ethical principle was advocated by Mencius: "The great man (a profoundly moral person) need not keep his word nor does he necessarily see his action through to the end. He aims only at what is right."[2] We are about to embark on the study of an ethico-religious tradition which so delicately shifts the moral focus from abstract principles to lived realities that it challenges many of our familiar categories in the comparative study of ethics and religion. Are we isolated individuals, or do we live as a center of interpersonal relationships? Is moral self-knowledge necessary for personal growth? Can any society prosper or endure without developing a basic sense of duty and responsibility among its members? Should our pluralistic society deliberately cultivate shared values and a common ground of human understanding? As we become acutely aware of our earth's vulnerability and increasingly wary of our own fate as an "endangered species," what are the critical spiritual questions we must ask? What would it mean for us to be happy?

The fundamental concern of the Confucian tradition is learning to be human. The focus is not on the human in contrast with nature or with Heaven but the human that seeks harmony with nature and mutuality with Heaven. Indeed, learning to be human, in the Confucian perspective, entails a broadening and deepening process that acknowledges the interconnectedness of all those ways which define the human condition. Through an ever-expanding network of relationships encompassing the family, community, nation, world, and beyond, the Confucian seeks to realize humanity in its all-embracing fullness. This process of inclusion helps deepen our self-knowledge at the same time through a ceaseless effort to make our body healthy, our mind-and-heart alert, our soul pure, and our spirit brilliant. Self-cultivation is an end in itself and its primary purpose is self-realization. That is what it means to be happy.

A defining characteristic of Confucian humanism is faith in the creative transformation of our human condition as a communal act and as a dialogical response to Heaven. This involves the integration of four dimensions of humanity: self, community, nature, and Heaven. An exploration of Confucian spirituality must take into consideration (1) the self as creative transformation, (2) the community as a necessary vehicle for human flourishing, (3) nature as the proper home for our form of life, and (4) Heaven as the source of ultimate self-realization.

I. SELF AS CREATIVE TRANSFORMATION

Confucius made it explicit that learning is for the sake of the self rather than for the sake of others.[3] On the surface, this seems to imply a sense of individuality fundamentally different from the conventional view of the primacy of the group in Confucian ethics. However, the Confucian insistence on learning for the sake of the self is predicated on the conviction that self-cultivation is an end in itself rather than a means to an end. Those who are committed to the cultivation of their personal life for its own sake can create inner resources for self-realization unimaginable to those who view self-cultivation merely as a tool for external goals such as social advancement and political success. While we are obligated to assume social responsibility and participate in political affairs, it is self-cultivation, as the root, securely grounding us in our life-world, that enables us to participate in society and politics as independent moral agents rather than as pawns in a game of power relationships. If we do not take self-realization seriously, we may easily allow ourselves to be defined by power and wealth totally external to our inner resources and our personal sense of worth.

For the Confucians, a personal sense of worth is vitally important because their commitment to improving the world from within compels them to take the status quo as the point of departure for their spiritual journey. If they do not subscribe to the thesis that learning is primarily for self-improvement, the demand for social service will undermine the integrity of self-cultivation as a noble end in itself. Therefore, learning as character building is for the sake of self-realization. The self so conceived is an open system involved in continuous transformation. It is never a static structure. The idea of the self as a discrete entity, isolated from the world, is diametrically opposed to the Confucian self as an open, dynamic, and transformative process.

The Confucian self, rooted in personal worth, seeks to generate its inner resources for self-transformation. Self-transformation, the result of self-cultivation, signifies a process of self-realization. However, since the idea of selfhood devoid of communication with the outside world is alien to the Confucian tradition, Confucian self-transformation does not take the form of searching exclusively for one's own inner spirituality. Authentic self-transformation involves tapping spiritual resources from the cumulative symbolic tradition, the sympathetic resonance of society, the vital energy of nature, and the creative power of Heaven.

II. COMMUNITY AND HUMAN FLOURISHING

A distinctive feature of the Confucian spiritual orientation is the view that the human community is an integral part of our quest for self-realization. The idea of cutting loose from our primordial ties— ethnicity, gender, language, land, and other intractable realities of life—as a precondition for our salvation is not even considered in the Confucian tradition. Confucians are profoundly aware that we are embedded in this world and that our spiritual journey must begin at home, here and now. While the sense of embeddedness may impose a structural limitation on the range of possibilities we can realistically envision in our spiritual self-transformation, it does not inhibit us from shaping the form of life most appropriate to our human condition.

The Confucian proposal that we begin our spiritual journey at home is based on the strong belief that our self is experientially and practically a center of relationships. As a center of relationships, it constantly enters into communication with a variety of human beings. The significance of the other for our self-cultivation is evident because we rarely cultivate ourselves in isolation. It is through constant human interaction that we gradually learn to appreciate our selfhood as a transformative process. Indeed, our feelings, thoughts, and ideas are not necessarily our private properties. While they are intensely personal, they need not be private; they are often better thought of as sharable public goods. The willingness to share empowers us to generate a dynamic process of interchange first with members of our family and, then, with our neighborhood community and beyond.[4] Concentric circles of relationship move out from the self to family, community, country, world, and beyond. This broadening process is central to the Confucian project of self-cultivation. As the opening statement of the Confucian classic, the *Great Learning*, states:

> The ancients who wished to illuminate "brilliant virtue" all under Heaven first governed their states. Wishing to govern their states, they first regulated their families. Wishing to regulate their families, they first cultivated their personal lives. Wishing to cultivate their personal lives, they first rectified their hearts and minds. Wishing to rectify their hearts and minds, they first authenticated their intentions. Wishing to authenticate their intentions, they first refined their knowledge. The refinement of knowledge lay in the study of things. For only when things are studied is knowledge refined; only when knowledge is refined are intentions authentic; only when intentions are authentic are hearts and minds rectified; only when hearts and minds are rectified are personal lives cultivated; only when personal lives are cultivated are families regulated; only when families are regulated are states governed; only when states are governed is there peace all under Heaven. Therefore, from the Son of Heaven to the common people, all, without exception, must take self-cultivation as the root.[5]

This statement suggests not only a broadening but also a deepening process. The way that the community is "embodied" in our self-transformation implies a continuous interplay between an inclusive process and a penetrating awareness. The assumption is that the more we broaden ourselves to involve others, the more we are capable of deepening our self-awareness; our persistence in deepening our self-awareness is the basis for our fruitful interaction with an ever-expanding network of human relatedness.

III. NATURE AS HOME

The Confucian ideal of human flourishing is, strictly speaking, not anthropological and is certainly not anthropocentric. Man is not the measure of all things. Such an idea strikes the Confucians as parochial. The proper measure for humanity is cosmological as well as anthropological; indeed it is "anthropocosmic." In the order of things, nature provides not only sustenance for life but also an inspiration for sustainable life. Implicit in the course of nature—the alternations of day and night and the changes of the four seasons—is a lesson in the enduring pattern of transformation: regularity, balance, and harmony.

Human civilization through time has endured natural calamities such as floods and hurricanes, but, despite the hardships of survival, the Confucians find nature a hospitable environment for our existence. They feel fortunate to have been blessed with "Heaven's timeliness and Earth's efficaciousness" and with the "wind and water" essentially wholesome for good health. Nature is revered for its generosity and its grandeur. Its awe-inspiring presence enables us to appreciate the fecundity and sanctity of our "home":

> The sky before us is only this bright, shining mass; but when viewed in its unlimited extent, the sun, moon, stars, and constellations are suspended in it and all things are covered by it. The earth before us is but a handful of soil; but in its breadth and depth, it sustains mountains like Hua and Yueh without feeling their weight; contains the rivers and seas without letting them leak away, and sustains all things. The mountain before us is but a fistful of straw; but in all the vastness of its size, grass and trees grow upon it, birds and beasts dwell on it, and stores of precious

things [minerals] are discovered in it. The water before us is but a spoonful of liquid, but in all its unfathomable depth, the monsters, dragons, fishes, and turtles are produced in it, and wealth becomes abundant because of it.[6]

This sense of nature as home empowers the Confucians to find ultimate meaning in ordinary human existence, to cultivate a regularized, balanced, and harmonious lifestyle, and to unite what many other religions divide into "the secular" and "the sacred."[7]

IV. HEAVEN AS THE SOURCE OF ULTIMATE SELF-TRANSFORMATION

While radical transcendence, such as understanding God as the "wholly other," is absent in Confucian symbols, Heaven as a source for moral creativity, meaning of life, and ultimate self-transformation features prominently throughout the Confucian tradition. In this sense, all major Confucian thinkers are profoundly religious. While their ways of being religious are significantly different from those in organized religions such as Christianity, Buddhism, or Islam, their reverence for life, commitment to work, and dedication to ultimate self-transformation are based on a calling comparable in intensity of feeling and seriousness of purpose to any of the great world religions.

The Confucian calling presupposes that Heaven is omniscient and omnipresent, if not omnipotent. What we do here and now as human beings has implications for ourselves, for our human community, for nature, and for Heaven. We need not appropriate the Way of Heaven by departing from where we are here and now, but since the Way of Heaven is right here, near at hand, and inseparable from our ordinary daily existence, what we do in the confines of our home is not only anthropologically but also cosmologically significant. If we properly nurture our human way, we will never be estranged from the Way of Heaven. Indeed, as we learn to appreciate the richness of ordinary daily existence, we understand that the great mystery of life is inherent in our common experience of living, as if the secret code of the Way of Heaven is embedded in the human way.

However, our internal organic connectedness with the transcendent through our own personal experience makes us aware of our inadequacy as well as our strength because we are charged with the awesome responsibility of realizing Heaven's Way through our humble human endeavors. The deepest meaning of humanity lies in its authentic manifestation as the guardian of nature and the cocreator of the cosmos:

> Only those who are absolutely sincere can fully develop their nature. If they can fully develop their nature, they can fully develop the nature of others. If they can fully develop the nature of others, they can then fully develop the nature of things. If they can fully develop the nature of things, they can then assist in the transforming and nourishing process of Heaven and Earth. If they can assist in the transforming and nourishing process of Heaven and Earth, they can thus form a trinity with Heaven and Earth.[8]

It is humanly possible to assist in the transforming and nourishing process of Heaven and Earth; it is authentically human to form a trinity with Heaven and Earth; and it is our categorical imperative to respond to Heaven's calling to serve as the guardian of nature and the cocreator of the cosmos.

Informed by the two major epochs of the Confucian tradition and the core values embodied in the Confucian sacred texts, we may wonder what significance this distinctively Confucian spiritual orientation really has. It should be obvious that some of the ideas widely employed in religious studies are inadequate in dealing with the Confucian tradition. Virtually all familiar exclusive dichotomies have lost their explanatory power: spirit/matter, body/mind, sacred/profane, creator/creature, and transcendence/immanence. We need to develop a new method, formulate a new procedure, and cultivate new symbolic resources to meet the challenge.

A simple, if not simple-minded, way out is to exclude the Confucian tradition from a comparative study of religion. But confining ourselves to the spirit, the life of the mind, the sacred world, the power of the creator, and the transcendent dimension in our religious discourse leads to a one-sided picture of the religious life. A much more exciting intellectual enterprise is to explore the spirituality of matter, the embodiment of the mind, the possibility of regarding the secular as sacred, the creative and transformative potential in humanity, and the meaning of immanent transcendence. Still, the provocativeness of the Confucian spiritual orientation lies in its "religiosity," rather than in its humanness, this-worldliness, and immanence.

What distinguishes the Confucian approach to human flourishing is its emphasis on education—education as a form of learning, particularly "learning for the sake of oneself." Learning is conceived by the Confucians as a continuous holistic process of character building. The process involves an existential commitment to the task of self-realization through the conscientious cultivation of the "great body." This involves a continuing process of self-learning for the purpose of acquiring self-knowledge. Self-reflection and personal introspective examination are constantly practiced as part of the daily routine. The Confucian self, in this sense, is not a static structure but a dynamic ever-changing process.

The case of the seventeenth-century Confucian teacher, Sun Ch'i-feng (1584–1675), is illuminating. His continuous reflectiveness enabled him to detect lapses in word and deed when he celebrated his ninetieth birthday. With a touch of humor, he even remarked in front of his students that only after he had turned eighty did he realize his childishness in his seventies. The Confucian definition of an adult is someone who has taken the "becoming process" seriously and is, therefore, well on his or her way to maturity. However, since the process of learning to be human is ceaseless, maturing never ends. We can sharpen our understanding of this dimension of the Confucian project by applying this insight to the life history of Confucius himself. Before Confucius died at the age of seventy-three, he had remarked that he "could follow the dictates of my heart without overstepping the boundaries of right" at seventy.[9] This total harmony between what one is and what one ought to be has been identified by later Confucians as an awe-inspiring attainment: the fusion of necessity with spontaneity. Had Confucius enjoyed the longevity of the Buddha and lived to the ripe old age of eighty, would he have been involved in further self-improvement? Despite the strong belief that what Confucius had attained symbolizes the highest stage of human maturation, the consensus among Confucian followers is that of course, if he had lived longer, he would have continued his unceasing efforts to learn and improve himself so that he could provide further richness and nuances to his life. Such a question seems out of place in either the Christian or Buddhist context.

We may summarize the Confucian paradox as follows: ontologically every human being is inevitably a sage and existentially no human being can ever become a sage. To put it in personal terms, I am not what I ought to be but the resources for me to learn what I ought to be are embedded in the very structure of what I am. This paradox, that every person is a potential sage while actually the process of learning to be a sage is never-ending, forms the context in which the Confucian Way is to be pursued.

Another salient feature of the Confucian spiritual orientation is the commitment to the intrinsic reasonableness and meaningfulness of this world here and now. Nevertheless, this commitment, far from being an adjustment to the world or an acceptance of the status quo, is motivated by a steadfast determination to transform the world from within. The perception that what the world is falls short of what it ought to be enables the Confucian to maintain a critical distance from the established economic interests, political power, and social hierarchy of the time. The existential decision not to take flight from the world but to immerse oneself in the economic, political, and social affairs of the time compels the Confucian to continuously interact with those in power and wrestle with "mundane" issues of the "secular" order. With a strong sense of moral responsibility and often with a profound sense of human tragedy as well, true Confucians, like Confucius, do what they realistically know cannot be done. A fruitful way of approaching this vitally important and often misunderstood dimension of Confucian spirituality is to examine, in some detail, how Confucius actually defined himself in such matters. Whether Confucius was "a prosaic and parochial moralizer" and his collected conversations, the *Analects*, fragmentary and commonsensical, or "a thinker with an imaginative vision of man equal in its grandeur to any [major philosophical or religious tradition]"[10] depends on our assessment of this particular aspect of the Confucian legacy.

Confucius' self-understanding may serve as a starting point for our exploration. He characterized himself as a fellow human being with a Heaven-ordained mission to transmit the Way as an inexhaustible student and a tireless teacher. A fellow human being specifies Confucius' humanness as an irreducible reality of his existence. The following exchange in the *Analects* clearly shows his existential choice to participate in the human fellowship, even though the thought of detaching himself from the world was not only a real possibility but also a persistent temptation:

> Ch'ang-chu and Chieh-ni were cultivating their fields together. Confucius was passing that way and told [his disciple] Tzu-lu to ask them where the river could be forded. Ch'ang-chu said, "Who is the one holding the reins in the carriage?" Tzu-lu said, "It is K'ung Ch'iu [Confucius' given name]." "Is he the K'ung Ch'iu of Lu [Confucius' native state]?" "Yes." "Then he already knows where the river can be forded!" Tzu-lu asked Chieh-ni. Chieh-ni said, "Who are you sir?" Tzu-lu replied, "I am Chung-yu (given name of Tzu-lu)." "Are you a follower of K'ung Ch'iu of Lu?" "Yes." Chieh-ni said, "The whole world is swept as though by a torrential flood. Who can change it? As for you, instead of following one who flies from this man or that man, is it not better to follow those who flee the world all together?" And with that he went on covering the seed without stopping. Tzu-lu went to Confucius and told him about the conversation. Confucius was lost in thought for a while and said, "One cannot herd with birds and beasts. If I do not associate with mankind, with whom shall I associate? If the Way prevailed in the world, there would be no need for me to change it."[11]

This exchange vividly portrays the encounter of two significantly different approaches to life. The hermits Ch'ang-chu and Chieh-ni opted to abdicate their social responsibility and "flee the world all together." While it would perhaps be inaccurate to characterize them as Taoists, their challenge to Confucius was unmistakably Taoistic. Confucius seems to have accepted their assessment of the objective conditions of their day: "the whole world is swept away as though by a torrential flood." He himself characterized the situation this way: "The phoenix does not come; the river chart does not emerge."[12] Yet, his personal decision about how to confront the disorders of his day differed radically from most men. The Taoists endeavored to cultivate their own piece of "pure land" so that they could enjoy a personal sense of tranquillity and unity with nature. They perceived with an ironic detachment people like Confucius who made desperate, and always abortive, attempts to right the wrongs of the world. They themselves, not unlike Thomas More with his utopian view of the mundane world, determined that politics had degenerated to the point of no return. To them, Confucius' "fleeing from this man or that man," which obviously referred to his frustrations with this or that ruler, was an exercise in futility.

The decision of Ch'ang-chu and Chieh-ni to sever their relationship with mankind was laden with far-reaching ethical and spiritual implications. In their view, the only hope for personal fulfillment in an age of disorder was to ignore the world's problems and "tend one's own garden." Ch'ang-chu's seemingly sarcastic remark that Confucius already knew where the river could be forded signifies, in a deeper sense, that the river, the "torrential flood that is sweeping the whole world," is too dangerous to be forded at all. Chieh-ni's rhetorical question to Tzu-lu—"Is it not better to follow those who flee the world all together?"—can best be understood as a warning, indeed, as an invitation. In fact, Chieh-ni's question was prophetic, for Tzu-lu later lost his life in a political struggle.

Confucius knew what his Taoist critics had opted to do, or more appropriately, what they had chosen to become. The Taoist choice actually appealed to him as a highly desirable style of life. Confucius himself once expressed a wish "to go and live among the nine wild tribes of the east"[13] and jokingly stated that if the Way did not prevail, he would "get upon a raft, and float about on the sea."[14] Confucius' fascination with music, his sensitivity to nature, and his delight in the simple pleasures of life[15] can all be cited to show that he was not, by temperament, out of tune with the Taoist vision. But for Confucius, it was precisely the nature of the times—the turmoil and disorder—that called for political engagement rather than detachment. There is pathos in his lamentation, "If the Way prevailed in the world, there would be no need for me to change it." His audacious personal assumption of the moral responsibility to change the world, to "repossess the Way,"[16] aroused much excitement, and also much suspicion, on the part of many people. A brief encounter with the "Madman of Ch'u" was not untypical:

> Chieh Yu, the Madman of Ch'u, went past Confucius, singing,
> Phoenix, oh phoenix! / How thy virtue has declined!
> What is past is beyond help,

What is to come is not yet lost.
Give up, give up!
Perilous is the lot of those in office today.
Confucius got down from his carriage with the intention of speaking
with him, but the Madman avoided him by hurrying off, and in the
end Confucius was unable to speak with him.[17]

The Madman of Ch'u was obviously impressed by the dangerous nature of Confucius' self-assigned mission. Others were equally
impressed by its apparent impracticality:

When Tzu-lu was stopping at the Stone Gate for the night, the
gatekeeper asked him, "Where are you from?" Tzu-lu said,
"From Confucius." "Oh, is he the one who knows that it cannot
be done and still does it?"[18]

In other words, in the awkward but accurate translation of James
Legge, he "knows the impractical nature of the times, and yet he will
be doing in them,"[19] because his sense of mission urges him on.

The seemingly contradictory description of Confucius' critical
awareness of the impracticality of putting his way into practice, and
his self-conscious resoluteness to carry it out with all his heart, per-
ceptively captures the spirit of the Confucian project. By inextricably
linking his own fortune with the whole world, even though he realistically understood that he could do very little to prevent the world
from being swept away by a torrential flood, he still chose to do the
best he could to show the Way of avoiding such an impending disas-
ter. This may have been an exercise in futility, especially if we apply
pragmatic criteria to assess his success in the political arena. However,
despite pessimistic talk about a world beyond redemption, Confucius'
faith in the transformability and perfectibility of human nature was
never in question. However bleak the immediate situation may have
appeared to him, he believed the Way could still prevail in society,
and even in politics, through education. In any case, he saw the great
task of "repossessing the Way" as a Heaven-ordained moral imperative and a spiritual calling, not to be denied whatever the odds.

We should also note that, despite Confucius' this-worldly spiritual
orientation, he was not exclusively concerned with the improvement of
the secular order. To characterize Confucius as a social reformer is
deceptively simplistic. The Confucian project has a transcendent

dimension. The idea that the human Way is sanctioned by Heaven implies that Confucian this-worldliness is profoundly religious. The religiousness of Confucius' mission as a "social reformer" is exemplified in a passage in the *Analects* about a border guard at Yi, in the state of Wei:

> The border official of Yi requested an audience, saying, "I have never been denied an audience by any nobleman who has come to this place." The followers presented him. When he came out, he said, "What worry have you, gentlemen, about the loss of office. The empire has long been without the Way. Heaven is about to use your Master as the wooden tongue for a bell [to rouse the Empire]."[20]

Suggestively, Confucius himself interpreted his own mission in transcendent terms. Once when Huan T'ui, the Minister of War in the state of Sung, attempted to kill him, he commented on the incident with unusual self-assurance: "Heaven is author of the virtue that is in me. What can Huan T'ui do to me?"[21] This seemingly presumptuous self-description signifies a deep-rooted commitment to the Way as a Heaven-ordained mission:

> When under siege in K'uang, the Master said, "With King Wen dead, is not culture (*wen*) invested here in me? If Heaven intends this culture to be destroyed, those who come after me will not be able to have any part of it. If Heaven does not intend this culture to be destroyed, then what can the men of K'uang do to me?"[22]

It would be misleading, however, if the transcendent dimension of the Confucian project were interpreted to mean that the course of culture, or the Way, would eventually prevail on its own. Confucius made it explicit: "It is the human that can make the Way great, and not the Way that can make the human great."[23] At the same time, as a mere human mortal, he also realized how difficult it was to live up to the demands of the Way of Heaven, and he was the first to admit his own shortcomings in this regard:

> There are four things in the Way of the profound person, none of which I have been able to do. To serve my father as I would expect my son to serve me: that I have not been able to do. To serve my ruler as I would expect my ministers to serve me: that

I have not been able to do. To serve my elder brothers as I would expect my younger brothers to serve me: that I have not been able to do. To be the first to treat friends as I would expect my friends to treat me: that I have not been able to do.[24]

The tension and conflict between his sense of mission—that he was entrusted by Heaven to transmit the Way—and his sense of deficiency "in practicing the ordinary virtues and in the exercise of care in ordinary conversation"[25] generated a dynamism in Confucius' "earnest and genuine" effort to learn fully to be human. This dynamism made him an inexhaustible student and an untiring teacher: "To remember silently [what I have learned], to learn untiringly, and to teach others without being wearied—that is just natural to me."[26] What drew people to this teacher was a quiet charisma embodied in his daily interactions with students. There was no prophetic claim of privileged access to the divine. Nor was there any suggestion of noble birth or superior native intelligence. Yet he aroused the devotion of his followers with the magic quality of his sincerity and authenticity:

> Shu-sun Wu-shu made defamatory remarks about Chung-ni [Confucius]. Tzu-kung said, "He is simply wasting his time. Chung-ni cannot be defamed. In other cases, men of excellence are like hills which one can climb over. Chung-ni is like the sun and the moon which one has no way of climbing over. Even if someone wanted to cut himself off from them, how could this detract from the sun and the moon? It would merely serve the more to show that he did not know his own measure."[27]

What inspired such devotion and confidence in his followers? Certainly they seem to have been heartened by his vision of the transcendent embedded in the practical living of ordinary daily existence. Moreover the commonness, humility, and reverence with which he approached life along with his burning conviction that steady improvement in human life is both a possibility and a necessity seem to have inspired many of them. Confucius may have failed as a potential statesman or as a practical social reformer. As an inspiring witness to the possibilities of human life, however, he certainly lived up to the calling of a fellow human being with a Heaven-ordained mission to transmit the Way, as an inexhaustible student and an untiring teacher.

So the personality of Confucius symbolizes a deep faith in the intrinsic worth of humanity. We may well ask ourselves whether such a seemingly naive faith can still be relevant to our problem-riddled world of the late twentieth century. To be sure, we are today constantly threatened by annihilation as a result of human wickedness, or, if you will, sinfulness. But in the Confucian view, the human condition can be improved and society can be transformed because human nature is forever improvable. There is a sense of duty that springs from the knowledge that we are irrevocably embedded in life on this earth. If we do not care for our home here, there is no other home to escape to. There is not even an afterlife to anticipate if we fail to live our lives morally, meaningfully, and fully on this earth here and now. Confucius asks that we take ourselves, and our lives here and now, absolutely seriously. We learn to be human neither to please the world nor to meet the expectations of our parents, but for the sake of ourselves as improvable human beings.

At the same time, since we are not isolated individuals, we should not choose to be loners. Robinson Crusoe's life of isolation is exhilarating to many of us not because of his solitude and independence, but because he demonstrated hope and perseverance. Confucians may think highly of these admirable human qualities, but they strongly believe that the dignity, autonomy, and independence of the person need not be based on individualism. To define our personhood or our selfhood in terms of human fellowship with others does not undermine our individuality but instead recognizes the self-evident truth that human beings reach their highest potential through communication and communal participation with other human beings.

Confucian humanism advocates that the world is redeemable through human effort, and that we can fully realize ourselves, or attain ultimate salvation, by self-cultivation. The Confucian view of personal development can be visualized as an open-ended series of concentric circles, because the Confucian idea of the self is not built on the idea of individuality as the core of the person, as is the Judeo-Christian sense of the soul or the Hindu sense of *atman*. Rather, in Confucianism, the self is always understood as the center of relationships. This open-ended series of concentric circles points to an ever-extending horizon. A person's growth and development should never be viewed as a lonely struggle, for it involves participation in a large context of human-relatedness. Moreover, this process of learning to be human is not simply the development of the self in relation to one's family, neighborhood, community, or state; it is also a deepening process of self-knowledge and self-understanding.

The point of departure for building a moral life through Confucian education is first to discipline the body. The six arts that constitute Confucian education—ritual, music, marksmanship, horsemanship, calligraphy, and mathematics—can all be understood as forms of training the body. Teaching young children, often beginning at the age of eight, to learn how to handle their bodies is not a trivial matter. In the case of ritual, it is extremely complicated and important to teach children the proper way to walk, to use their hands, to sit, and to answer simple questions. This ritualization of the body in which youngsters eventually learn the ritual language to express themselves, enables them to participate in the larger human community and to communicate meaningfully through their bodily movements as well as words and ideas.

The notion of *shen-chiao*, often translated as "exemplary teaching," literally means "body teaching"—teaching through the example of the body rather than simply teaching by words. The teachers, through personal exemplification, induce the students to emulate them as standards of inspiration rather than mechanistic models. In fact the Confucian *Analects* contain many interesting examples of this kind. The modern reader may find it difficult to appreciate some of the descriptions of how Confucius presented gifts, taught, ate, visited a temple, or how he performed simple mundane acts. These may seem to many to be conventional descriptions of ordinary behavior, but the message of the *Analects* is to present Confucius as a living person in the context of human-relatedness and in the process of ritualizing his own body.

Confucius' concern with ritual, with "learning to be human," and with "repossessing and transmitting the Way," suggests a critical awareness that cultural creativity necessarily involves accepting certain aspects of the past to emulate in the present. Creating something out of nothing is not the paradigm of creativity for the Confucian. Rather, creativity in the cultural arena entails interpretive brilliance. It is in this sense that Confucius characterized himself as a transmitter rather than the creator of a tradition. While Confucius was not the founder of the *Ju* tradition, he revived and reinvigorated it, through his personal act of interpretation, to the extent that the *Ju* tradition is synonymous with the Confucian Way, the Way of achievable human happiness.

NOTES

I gratefully acknowledge the kind permission of Harper San Francisco to include excerpts from my chapter on "Confucianism" in *Our Religions*, ed. Arvind Sharma (San Francisco: Harper San Francisco, 1993). It should be noted that the presentation of the excerpted material in the Boston University Institute for Philosophy and Religion lecture series predated the publication of my chapter in *Our Religions*. I am indebted to Leroy S. Rouner and Barbara Darling-Smith for their guidance and patience in the development of this essay.

1. *Analects* 14.34.

2. *Mencius* IVB:11. See *Mencius*, trans. D. C. Lau, 2 vols. (Hong Kong: Chinese University Press, 1984), 1:163.

3. *Analects* 14.24.

4. Tu Wei-ming, "Embodying the Universe: A Note on Confucian Self-Realization," in Tu Wei-ming, *Confucian Thought: Selfhood as Creative Transformation* (Albany, N.Y.: State University of New York Press, 1991), p. 175.

5. *The Great Learning*, chap. 1. Cf. Daniel K. Gardner, *Chu Hsi and the Ta-hsueh: Neo-Confucian Reflection on the Confucian Canon* (Cambridge, Mass.: Council on East Asian Studies, Harvard University, 1986), pp. 88–94.

6. *The Doctrine of the Mean (Chung-yung)*, chap. 26. See Wing-tsit Chan, trans. and comp., *A Source Book in Chinese Philosophy* (Princeton: Princeton University Press, 1973), p. 109. For *tien*, "sky," rather than "heaven," is used in this translation.

7. An expression borrowed from Herbert Fingarette, *Confucius: The Secular as Sacred* (New York: Harper & Row, 1972).

8. *Doctrine of the Mean*, chap. 22. See Chan, *Source Book in Chinese Philosophy*, pp. 107–8. Singular pronouns ("he") have been replaced by the plural ("they") in this translation.

9. *Analects* 2.4.

10. Fingarette, *Confucius*, p. vii.

11. *Analects* 18.6. For this translation, see Chan, *Source Book in Chinese Philosophy*, p. 48. While Chan translates *wu-jan* as "ruefully," in this particular case I follow D. C. Lau in rendering it as "lost in thought for a

while." See D. C. Lau, *Confucius: The Analects* (Harmondsworth, England: Penguin Books, 1979), p. 150. James Legge renders the same expression as "with a sigh." See James Legge, trans., *The Chinese Classics* (Oxford: Clarendon Press, 1883), 1:334.

12. *Analects* 9.8. The arrival of the phoenix and the emergence of the river chart were considered the auspicious signs of a peaceful age.

13. *Analects* 9.13. See Legge, *Chinese Classics*, 1:221.

14. *Analects* 5.6. See Legge, *Chinese Classics*, 1:174.

15. For some outstanding examples of this, see *Analects* 7.13, 6.21, and 7.15.

16. An expression used by William T. de Bary in conceptualizing the idea of *tao-t'ung* in the Confucian tradition. See W. T. de Bary, *The Liberal Tradition in China* (Hong Kong: Chinese University Press; and New York: Columbia University Press, 1983), p. 9.

17. *Analects* 18.5. See Lau, *Confucius: The Analects*, pp. 149–50.

18. *Analects* 14.41.

19. Legge, *Chinese Classics*, 1:290. D. C. Lau is more explicit in his rendering of the same passage: "Is that the K'ung who keeps working towards a goal the realization of which he knows to be hopeless?" See Lau, *Confucius: The Analects*, p. 130. It should be noted that in Lau's translation this saying is classified as XIV:38 instead of 14.41.

20. *Analects* 3.24. See Lau, *Confucius: The Analects*, p. 71.

21. *Analects* 7.23. See Lau, *Confucius: The Analects*, p. 89.

22. *Analects* 9.5. See Lau, *Confucius: The Analects*, p. 96.

23. *Analects* 15.28. See Chan, *Source Book in Chinese Philosophy*, p. 44.

24. *Doctrine of the Mean*, chap. 13. See Chan, *Source Book in Chinese Philosophy*, p. 101. For a brief discussion on this, see Tu Wei-ming, *Centrality and Commonality: An Essay on Chung-yung* (Honolulu: University Press of Hawaii, 1976), pp. 37–45.

25. *Doctrine of the Mean*, chap. 13. See Chan, *Source Book in Chinese Philosophy*, p. 101.

26. *Analects* 7.2. See Chan, *Source Book in Chinese Philosophy*, p. 31.

27. *Analects* 19.24. See Lau, *Confucius: The Analects*, p. 156.

PART III

Ecstasy, the Uneasy Conscience, Meaning, Playfulness

Ecstasy and Truth

LEROY S. ROUNER

I

SINCE THE RENAISSANCE, the common wisdom in Western culture has presupposed a radical difference between scientific and religious ways of knowing, based on the differing objects of knowledge (nature and God), the way that knowledge is received (reason and revelation), and the kind of language used to express it (philosophy and theology).

This distinction is further reflected in the means of knowledge. Scientific rationality has clear rules and genuine universality. We all agree that "2+2=4," or that "this particular rock is granite," and we all recognize the rational and empirical rules by which we came to that conclusion. There is therefore nothing mysterious, or weird, or hidden, about such scientific affirmations, no matter what one's ethnic, cultural, or religious background. The affirmation is thoroughly *exoteric* and publicly available. Scientific reason is therefore a natural ally of both democracy and common sense. Religion, on the other hand, regularly appeals to "revelation," a means of knowledge which is "beyond reason," and is open only to those who have had this distinctive experience. Religious reason is therefore *esoteric;* a natural ally of secrecy, and of aristocracies. Or so the common wisdom holds.

My argument, in opposition to the common wisdom, is that there is a critical point at which scientific ways of knowing and religious ways of knowing are comparable. That point comes when one asks how one can know that the basic principles which undergird one's knowledge are actually true. These basic principles are what Aristotle calls the *archai* of any science. To make that argument I have chosen to compare the views of Aristotle and Tillich on knowledge of first principles. My argument has two purposes. The first is modest, and admittedly defensive. I want to counter the view that religious appeals to a nonrational revelation are necessarily irrational. I do this by analyzing a precedent in Aristotle, who also appeals to nonrational (but not irrational) ways of knowing in order to establish the truth of the *archai* of science. To be sure, while this view may be characteristic of Greek thought, it has not found favor in modern Western philosophy, where the "truth question" is thoroughly vexed. But that whole discussion is much too complex and extensive to attempt here. I shall be content if my modest observation is clear, and delighted if it is persuasive.

The second purpose is hopefully more interesting. I suggest that Tillich has provided a more imaginative analysis than Aristotle of the way we come to know that the first principles of our knowledge are true. This analysis comes in the unlikely context of Tillich's doctrine of "ecstatic reason." Despite its romantic overtones, it seems to me to say something which Aristotle needs to say but which he does not develop.

II

In the *De Anima* Aristotle understands *nous,* the power of knowing, as functional and dynamic. It is functional in that it is always an operation within a specific context. *Nous* is capacity or potentiality exercised in the process of knowing whatever is known. And it is always dynamic, because the power of *nous* is activated by "desire" in response to an object. This desired object "moves" the power of *nous* to know it. In causing the mind to desire to know it, however, the object of desire is not changed itself. It moves something else, but is not itself moved; it is an "unmoved mover." As a factor in the knowing process it stimulates that process, and is the point toward which the process is directed. On the other hand, it is outside the process because it is not affected by it.[1]

For human conduct and action the highest intellectual excellence for Aristotle is practical intelligence, which he equates with art, and which John Hermann Randall, Jr., identifies with "what we Americans have come to call 'know-how.'"[2] But both practical intelligence and art differ from theoretical wisdom, a combination of science, or demonstration from first principles (*archai*), and *nous,* which must finally evaluate and authenticate these *archai. Nous,* as theoretical wisdom, thus deals with universals, things that always are, and cannot be other than they are. But *nous,* for Aristotle, is regularly "passive," in that the universal acts upon it in producing knowledge. Two points are significant here. One is that *nous* exists only in the act of *nousing*. The other is that *nous* has no structure, because it is potentially all universals. As pure potentiality it is possible to know things as they really are, without an intermediary (and distorting) structure.

Here, of course, Aristotle's realism and naturalism is at odds with most post-Kantian Western philosophy, where knowledge is made possible by the interpreting and constructive capacities of thought. For Aristotle, knowing is a transaction which takes place in an intelligible world, when the power of the subject to know conjoins with the power of the object to be known. Sensations are not a barrier between the mind and the world of objects for Aristotle, as they later were for Locke, because he regards them as the natural means by which the mind knows its natural world. For modern philosophy, on the other hand, knowing is a transaction which takes place in the mind of the knower, when percepts are turned into concepts. Experience must therefore be a construct, because the world, *qua* world, is not inherently intelligible. The world becomes intelligible only when the mind interprets and reconstructs experience. But this intelligibility is in the mind of the knower, not in the world. In this context the "truth question" regarding the first principles of any science is almost impossible to frame, much less to solve; and philosophizing takes place under the threatening shadow of solipsism. For Aristotle, on the other hand, *nous* makes it possible for us to know an intelligible world as it really is.

But for this to be true, knowing must be separable from the body and its qualities, its structures and especially its limitations.[3] Given his functionalism and contextualism, however, this separability presents a problem for Aristotle. *Nous* is to be understood in relation to its desired objects, the universals. And while these universals are not separate from matter, since a universal is always *of* something, we can conceive them as so, in the same way that we can conceive mathematical objects, such as a curve, as separable from curved objects in our experienced world. We can speak of "a curve" as though it could exist independently of curve balls, the snubness of Socrates' nose, etc.; even though, for Aristotle, the universal is real only as the meaning of "curve" in our experience of particulars. Yet how, Aristotle asks, is it possible for the separated *nous* to think, since thinking is a being acted upon? How is it possible for it to know itself, if it has no structure or nature of its own?

His response is not entirely clear. There is the brief and famous paragraph in *De Anima* which later interpreters described as his doctrine of the "active intellect," in which he states that there is a dimension of mind which transcends its passivity, one in which mind is "a sort of positive state like light" and is "in its essential nature activity."[4] Werner Jaeger, A. E. Taylor, John H. Randall, Jr., and others have argued that this is a fragmentary remnant from his younger "Platonic" thinking, and that the "active intellect" is not a significant part of *De Anima*. Be that as it may, it is relevant to the issue of how we know that the first principles of a science are true. In the *Posterior Analytics* he concludes that "there can be no scientific knowledge of primary premisses, and since except intuition nothing can be truer than scientific knowledge, it will be intuition that apprehends the primary premisses."[5] This intuition is, as for Plato, a kind of "seeing," or recognition. It is an exercise of intelligence; or, as Randall used to say to his students, it is like getting the point of a joke. But surely this is a weak "explanation," and says little more than that we do indeed somehow seem to know it.

The doctrine of the "active intellect" *does* provide an explanation, but such a mind would constitute the "Unmoved Mover" of the world's intelligibility—that is, the divine mind—and that "religious" affirmation is counter to the spirit and most of the content of Aristotle's naturalism. Randall—himself a naturalist—suggests that Aristotle's problem is that of any naturalistic theory of knowing and intelligence, which tries to stick to the facts.

> If we grant "knowing" to be a fact—if we hold that intelligence is not merely an organ of adjustment and adaptation, but a means of arriving at what may fairly be called "truth"—then mind does seem to rise above the limitations and conditions of its bodily instrument, and to be, as Aristotle puts it, "unmixed and separable," and in its vision "deathless and eternal." This is Plato's insight. It is not so much a theory about the ontological status of *nous*, as an appreciation of what *nous* can do.[6]

If one holds with the "Platonizing" interpretations of Aristotle, the "active intellect" is the cosmic *Nous*, or God, which "illuminates" the "passive intellect" of humankind. The result is a view happily at home with many Christian doctrines of "revelation," in which the mind of God "illuminates" our minds. But that is probably claiming too much. At the very least, however, Aristotle is clear that our confirming knowledge of the *archai* of any science cannot be "scientific" knowledge, but must be something even more certain, an "intuitive" grasp of truth. Such nonscientific knowledge is nonrational, but not irrational, since it is the cornerstone of science and all rational knowledge. The unresolved issue is how *nous* can actually be "unmixed and separable" in the act of "intuiting" the truth of *archai*. This is an issue which Tillich explores in his doctrine of "ecstatic reason."

III

The problem for Tillich's doctrine of "Reason and the Quest for Revelation" is that he needs an epistemology which is both modern and classical.[7] He is a post-Kantian philosopher who understands experience as constituted by interpretation and construction, what he calls the "grasping and shaping" powers of reason, in contrast to Aristotle's characteristically Greek understanding of reason as passive. At the same time, as a philosophical theologian, Tillich needs a conception of human logos which can provide a bridge to the divine Logos, the "Word" of God. So he proposes "Two Concepts of Reason."[8] One is modern: "technological reason" is the individual human capacity for "reasoning." It is instrumental and operational, in the spirit of American pragmatism. The other is "ontological reason," which is reason as "the structure of the mind."

He conjoins these two by arguing that "according to the classical tradition, reason is the structure of the mind which enables the mind to grasp and to transform reality."[9] While the statement is historically misleading, this view makes it possible for Tillich to integrate the two conceptions. Schelling's German idealism here joins hands with Dewey's American pragmatism. "Grasping and shaping" is what we moderns must do; but we can do it only because this function is grounded in the ontological structures of the mind recognized by German idealists and the classical Greek conception of reason. "Neither structures, Gestalt processes, values, nor meaning can be grasped without ontological reason."[10] "Subjective reason"—the rational structure of the mind—is therefore related to "objective reason"—the rational structure of reality. Tillich suggests four ways of conceiving this relationship—realism, idealism, dualism, and monism—but, *qua* theologian, makes no judgment about them. What is significant for our purposes, however, is his existentialism.

Rational activity always involves both continuity and change, and for Tillich both the static and dynamic elements of reason are subject to "existential distortion." This is a far cry from Aristotle's view that knowing is a natural function in a naturally intelligible world. Aristotle took it for granted that we know. His philosophical task was simply to analyze how that process works. Tillich, on the other hand, inherits the modern "problem of knowledge," which requires an explanation of how we can really know anything at all. This existential distortion is partly because "an emotional element is present in every rational act."[11] But more importantly, reason is actual only in the processes of being, existence and life; and "Being is finite, existence is self-contradictory, and life is ambiguous."[12] Tillich, following Plato, argues that actual existence is "fallen" from the realm of essence, which is its true nature. Although Tillich does not use the metaphor, "existential distortion" is his version of the *skia*, or "shadows" of reality which is all experience provides in the *Republic*'s "myth of the cave." How, then, is it possible to have any objective knowledge? And especially, how is it possible to "know that my Redeemer liveth"?

Aristotle's answer to the question about the foundations of knowledge is that we "intuit" their truth. While this is not an explanation, it is viable in Aristotle's philosophy because he has previously established how the mind has true knowledge of its experienced world. His "intuition" is an extrapolation from this scientific knowledge of the world. Tillich, following Nicolaus Cusanus' doctrine of "learned ignorance" and Kant's doctrine of "critical ignorance," argues that actual reason cannot escape finitude. This is not radically opposed to Aristotle's views on how we know our experienced world, since the experience which reason seeks to understand is initially that of a finite world anyway.

The distinction between the two comes when the foundational question arises. Aristotle wants to maintain the integrity of *nous*, even though there must be a dimension of *nous*, or a moment in the process of knowing, when *nous* is "separable" from its normally passive condition. The difference between Aristotle and Tillich is that for Tillich, there is a limit to the power of *nous*, when something distinctively different comes into play. Aristotle toyed with the notion of an "active intellect" as a solution to his problem, but then drew back. Tillich presents a theory of how the divine mind illuminates our minds. But this is to get ahead of the argument.

The "ignorance" noted in both Cusanus and Kant is of something which reason reaches for but cannot grasp, and that is its own foundations. Again, Tillich is not radically different from Aristotle at this point. Both recognize that *nous* needs a new dimension in order to establish its own foundations. Tillich uses a metaphor—"the depth of reason"— to name a "power and meaning" which is manifest in actual reason, but which "precedes" it. "The depth of reason is its quality of pointing to truth-itself, namely, to the infinite power of being and of the ultimately real, through the relative truths in every field of knowledge."[13] This, too, is Aristotelian. But Tillich, committed to both classical and modern views, elaborates a dialectical understanding. This "reaching out" of reason, its "quest," derives from the polarity within actual reason between its structure and its "depth." This leads to a conflict between what Tillich calls "autonomy and heteronomy under the conditions of existence," and leads to the "quest for theonomy."

Tillich has partly revived ("autonomy" and "heteronomy") and partly invented ("theonomy") a distinctive philosophical jargon which needs definition. Autonomous reason is what he has earlier referred to as "technical reason." This is reason as instrument, "reasoning" in the modern world of autonomous individuals, whereby we interpret and shape our immediate world of experience. It is reason which "affirms and actualizes its structure without regarding its depth."[14] *Heteronomy* ("strange law") is more complicated, because its relationship to autonomy is both "outside" and "inside." Autonomous reason seeks freedom from the restraints of heteronomy, which imposes its law from outside, but it does so in the name of the depth of reason, which autonomy has forsaken.

These are difficult concepts, because Tillich is very abstract, seldom offering illustrations. An example, however, would be the struggle within the Roman Catholic Church between "modernist" tendencies (autonomy) and the authority of the hierarchy (heteronomy). In conflict with a shallow autonomy, heteronomy seeks to speak in an unconditional way for the "ground" of being-itself, or for truth-itself. This is a tragic conflict within reason itself, since reason requires both the freedom of autonomy and the grounding of heteronomy. So the existential conflict within actual reason seeks a resolution and integration in what Tillich calls "theonomy," the creative law of the divine mind, in which autonomous reason reestablishes its ground.

For Aristotle the "unmixed and separable" *nous* is "divine"—or, perhaps better, "transcendent"—in that it conjoins the intelligibility of our minds with the intelligibility of the cosmic *Nous* itself. Aristotle's naturalism shows no interest in religion, but—as the difficult issue of the "active intellect" in *De Anima* indicates—he has either said too much or not enough on the issue of transcendent knowing. Randall suggests that he said too much. I think he didn't say enough. If, indeed, human knowing is capable of a vision which is "deathless and eternal," that fact is of great philosophical significance, and ought to be explored. Because he is a theologian Tillich cannot avoid a philosophical analysis of transcendent knowing. Whether his analysis would make Aristotle happy is another matter. But at least Tillich has an interesting view of how we can "intuit" the cosmic *Nous*.

As a Christian, Tillich needs to distinguish between the transcendent/divine mind and our minds, since God cannot "save" us unless God is, in some sense, different from us. So human reason is not "divine," but it does know the divine. This knowledge is "revelation." That is to say, the activating energy flows not from our "active intellect" but from the "Unmoved Mover" to us. For Tillich the cosmic *Nous* is different from the human *nous*, but *nous* in us has the capacity to receive this transcendental reality because it can "stand outside" itself. Or, as Aristotle puts it, our *nous* is capable of being "separable" and "unmixed" in relation to the ordinary functions of human knowing.

Tillich begins by pointing out that the transcendental reality to be known is "mysterious." There is theological content to this idea which need not concern us here. On the philosophical side, this encounter with mystery drives reason beyond itself to that which precedes it, its depth, "to the fact that 'being is and nonbeing is not' (Parmenides), to the original fact (*Urtatsache*) that there is *something* and not *nothing*."[15] In Aristotle's terms this is only to recognize that a vision of the "deathless and eternal" is obviously something which cannot be approached through our ordinary ways of knowing, because nothing in our world of experience is "deathless and eternal." Tillich adds that a genuine mystery cannot lose its mysteriousness, even when it is "revealed." That is to say, to know the "deathless and eternal" is precisely to "know" something that is "beyond knowing" because it is unlike anything we can ordinarily know.

It is possible to "know" this mystery, however, because of the possibility of "ecstasy," which Tillich defines as "standing outside oneself," and which is not unlike Aristotle's notion of a condition in which mind is "unmixed and separable." Tillich argues that it "points to a state of mind which is extraordinary in the sense that the mind transcends its ordinary situation." Ecstasy is not a negation of reason; it is the state of mind in which reason is beyond itself, that is, beyond the subject-object structure. In being beyond itself reason does not deny itself. "'Ecstatic reason' remains reason; it does not receive anything irrational or antirational—which it could not do without self-destruction—but it transcends the basic condition of finite rationality, the subject-object structure. . . . Ecstasy occurs only if the mind is grasped by the mystery, namely, by the ground of being and meaning. And, conversely, there is no revelation without ecstasy."[16]

Tillich is eager to distinguish his use of ecstasy from popular religious usage because ecstatic movements tend to put heavy emphasis on the emotional content of ecstasy. He admits that ecstatic experience necessarily has a subjective side, and that ecstasy therefore always has emotional content. This is also true, of course, for the philosopher who has a vision of the "deathless and eternal." This is always at least an "Aha!" experience; to have this "intuition" without excitement is impossible. But Tillich is primarily concerned with the objective side of ecstasy. It transcends the psychological level of experience. In so doing, "it reveals something valid about the relation between the mystery of our being and ourselves."[17]

What takes us out of ourselves in this ecstatic experience is what Tillich calls "ontological shock." What he has to say about it is colored with romanticism and existentialism, neither of which are characteristic of Aristotle. On the other hand, a vision of the "deathless and eternal" not only has to be emotionally exciting; it has to be metaphysically reorienting/disorienting. Such a vision would be literally "awesome." To encounter the cosmic *Nous*, wherein being and meaning are revealed as deathless and eternal, is, for Tillich, also to confront the possibility of nonbeing and to experience the power of the classical query, "Why is there something and not nothing?" So he argues that "the threat of nonbeing, grasping the mind, produces the 'ontological shock' in which the negative side of the mystery of being—its abysmal element—is experienced. 'Shock' points to a state of mind in which the mind is thrown out of its normal balance, shaken in its structure. Reason reaches its boundary line, is thrown back on itself, and then is driven again to its extreme situation. This experience of ontological shock is expressed in the cognitive function by the basic philosophical question, the question of being and non-being. It is, of course, misleading if one asks with some philosophers: 'Why is there something? Why not nothing?' For this form of the question points to something that precedes being, from which being can be derived. But being can only be derived from being. The meaning of this question can be expressed in the statement that being is the original fact which cannot be derived from anything else. Taken in this sense, the question is a paradoxical expression of the ontological shock and, as such, the beginning of all genuine philosophy."[18]

Tillich takes pains to emphasize that ecstatic experience does not destroy the rational structure of the mind. What the "ontological shock" does do, however, is both to annihilate and to elevate our rational experience of self and world. It is annihilating in that the ecstatic experience of mind as "separable and unmixed" sets aside our ordinary rational experience. At the same time, this same experience elevates our *nous* to heady relationship with the cosmic *Nous*. Tillich uses the terminology which Rudolf Otto's *Idea of the Holy* made famous; this is the experience of *mysterium tremendum* and *mysterium fascinosum*.

Aristotle and Tillich have very different philosophical sensibilities, and they did their philosophizing in very different cultural contexts. Nevertheless, there are some fundamental questions which are relevant to philosophy in whatever age. Chief among these is how we know that our foundational principles are true. On such questions conversations between philosophers of science and philosophers of religion can at least be suggestive, perhaps even mutually helpful.

NOTES

1. Aristotle *De Anima* 3.9.

2. John Herman Randall, Jr., *Aristotle* (New York: Columbia University Press, 1960), p. 77.

3. "Therefore, since everything is a possible object of thought, mind in order, as Anaxagoras says, to dominate, that is to know, must be pure from

all admixture . . ." *De Anima* 3.4.429a18–20. All Aristotle quotations are from Richard McKeon, *The Basic Works of Aristotle* (New York: Random House, 1941).

4. Aristotle *De Anima* 3.5.430a15–20.

5. Aristotle *Posterior Analytics* 2.19.100b10–12.

6. Randall, *Aristotle*, p. 103.

7. Paul Tillich, *Systematic Theology*, vol. 1 (Chicago: University of Chicago Press, 1951), pp. 71–105.

8. Ibid., p. 71.

9. Ibid., p. 72.

10. Ibid., p. 73.

11. Ibid., p. 77.

12. Ibid., p. 81.

13. Ibid., p. 79.

14. Ibid., p. 83.

15. Ibid., p. 110.

16. Ibid., p. 111–12.

17. Ibid., p. 113.

18. Ibid.

Happiness and
the Uneasy Conscience

RUTH L. SMITH

IT IS THIS WORLD, with its multi-dimensions and aspects, that I want to defend in exploring the notion of happiness and the "uneasy conscience." In speaking about this topic I am largely addressing those of us whose vocation or avocation it is to reflect on our understandings of morality as part of the meaning and activity of human existence. The more general question I'm addressing is that of our moral discourse—what it assumes is going on in moral activity and the terms by which it accounts for it. I am saying that while moral theories are most often in the position of recommending what we should be doing to be moral, they are also describing a situation phenomenologically. This description may be more powerfully normative than the explicit prescription. Notions of happiness and "uneasiness" are a point at which to observe this problem. They invite us into the implicit discourse of reflection on morality, and one of the first things to notice is that happiness often makes people engaged in moral theory uneasy.

The "uneasy conscience" is Reinhold Niebuhr's phrase. I use it because I will use Niebuhr to help us explore relations between happiness and moral experience and reflection. Niebuhr uses the phrase to indicate the disjuncture between the self-satisfied liberal conscience and the kind of dissatisfied conscience nonliberal religion could critically bring to bear on liberal society. Niebuhr proposes a discourse of ambiguity, irony, and paradox to displace the liberal discourse of a rational life plan, free self-realization, and the natural harmony of interests and values. In doing so he argues not only for a different framework for activity in the world—one more related to power structures in individuals and societies—but also for a different attitude and outlook, a different way to be a moral adult.

Niebuhr thought that the events of the twentieth century were reason enough to argue for the disjuncture between happiness as liberals constructed it and morality as he constructed it. The events of the great depression, two world wars, the Nazis, the Holocaust, and Stalinism were for him sufficient grounds for rendering invalid the rationalist view of human nature and turning to a more sober, complex view of the human condition. Niebuhr believed that liberal happiness was based on illusions about inevitability of progress, the unambiguous goodness of freedom, and the benign course of reasoned self-interest.

Even if people do not accept all of Niebuhr's premises, they often share the suspicion about happiness that haunts his work. Indeed this suspicion is habitual among those who consider themselves critical thinkers. The world is such a terrible place that talk of happiness seems out of place, disrespectful and insensitive, possibly self-indulgent. The fear that happiness is based on illusion is also strong, in part fed by a hypersensitivity in critical thinking as we have defined it to the ironic and the angular, to all that is mismatched in life. The concern about illusion also involves a fear that what we like will turn on us. And it involves a keen awareness of the kinds of illusory happiness promoted in a society in which consumption has such power to define what happiness is and is not. Happiness seems counter to the critical mind which fears naivete and sentimentality by which one might be taken in, which fears illusion and looking foolish to oneself and others, and which fears that the detached, oppositional terms of moral judgment would be dangerously blurred by well-being, pleasure, and joy. Human happiness is difficult to talk about in moral theory. Happiness is not only elusive but we also fear that happiness will dull our sensibilities and make us less aware of what is going on in the world.

I am concerned about the problematic character of happiness in moral theory and the prohibition against a positive attachment to this world. I cluster the various expressions of this prohibition under the old rubric of world-renunciation. My argument is that notions of world rejection thread through many habitual aspects and outlooks of dominant moral theories, constituting a kind of prior decision that the world is a site of pollution and disvalue. Its pleasures are dangerous and its values degenerative. As such it must in some way be held at a distance. The establishment of the terms of distance and the consequent terms of negotiation back into the world becomes a primary aspect of moral theory, if not the definition of ethics itself. The negotiation involves sets of familiar dualisms that constitute the means of passage: real and ideal, perfection and compromise, disinterest and egotism, autonomy and heteronomy, self-sacrifice and self-interest, individual and society, love and justice.

You may immediately object that I have got it backwards and indeed I have only hinted at part of the story so far. What characterizes the moral theories of the modern period is their location in this world as the site of human activity and authority. The other-worldly orientation of world-renunciation would seem to belong to the pilgrims of the Middle Ages or the early Gnostics or the sectarian practices of groups such as the Amish or Mennonites. One of the legacies of the Enlightenment is the notion that human beings not only seek happiness but can become happy in this life—politically, economically, and morally. Happiness is not the province of the next world but of this one, a point on which Adam Smith and Karl Marx agreed. From their vantage point, the world and the human nature in it is remediable (Smith) or transformable (Marx) toward this end.

Liberalism is fraught with contradictions on this matter. Kierkegaard and Schleiermacher or Rawls and Nozick or Niebuhr and Rauschenbusch express in complex ways differing evaluations of just what can be made of human beings and just how settled in we potentially can be among ourselves in society. In a simplified way, we find two versions of liberalism here. In one version reason and freedom are the vehicles by which human beings make themselves at home in this world. The world is not only permeable by liberal categories and goals but it is coterminous with them. To the liberal way of thinking no other history or world exists but its own; or to put it another way, all worlds are potentially its own and inherently desirous of being so in order to share in its satisfactions.

In the other version, reason and freedom are the vehicles by which human beings experience the world as a site of alienation and homelessness. This version, to which Niebuhr gave decisive shape in this century, emphasizes the ambiguity of reason and freedom. The emphasis here is not on the permeability of human nature toward the good but on the perpetually resistant aspects of the ego's desire for power in all human activity, especially in public life. Reason and freedom are vehicles for the expression and securing of our self-interests and any achievement of individual and social good is a continuously uphill battle.

Historically these views have often criticized each other's politics with epithets of "utopic" and "reactionary." Theologians compare these views in terms of their notions of sin and evil, the first holding to the view of human beings working our way out of ignorance under conditions of available grace and the second holding to the view of human beings working under the indelible mark of sin. However, I would argue that these views are not so simply oppositional and the notion of world-renunciation helps us see that.

Both views require distance from the world in order to evaluate it morally and in setting the conditions of this distance both define the world as a place of pollution. The rejection of the world as a place of unbridled competition and greed is the more familiar version of renunciation. But the rationalist views of individuality also express renunciation in their strategies by which moral agency always takes place at a detached distance from the detrimental effects of relation and engagement. This second version is one Niebuhr finds optimistic and deluded because of its confidence in a rationalism detached from power. My point here is that a theme of negation occurs in both versions. Neither of them finds the world as world acceptable. One version finds that the world can never really be cleaned up; it is a perpetually dirty room that can be set to rights but never really set in good order. As such the world carries with it a residual unhappiness and alienation because we have a residual awareness of unreachable perfection. The other version finds that the world can be cleaned up if we exit the world to do so. By moving ourselves into a rationally constructed space apart from the world's relations, we can create right order.

Both views are also views of perfection. Initially it appears that perfection is potentially attainable in one but not in the other. Yet the perfection that might be available, understood as the perfection of reason, is attainable but at the cost of accepting the negation of the world. This negation has not appeared to be a high price to pay; indeed, it has seemed necessary or even natural. We have a legacy of dismissive distinctions about what perfection is and the world is not: contingent and non-contingent, impermanent and permanent, changeable and unchangeable. These distinctions are considered the very basis for doing ethics and conducting a moral life.

Those outside the realm of professional philosophy and religion are quick to see the negation that runs through much of our thinking.

The distinctions so important to those who think about morality by profession seem more like family squabbles to those who stand elsewhere. My students regularly bring the world-denying character of much of the Western philosophical and Christian tradition to my attention. This happened recently when Thomson Kneeland asked after the class discussion of the *Bhagavad Gita*, thinking also of Simone Weil and Kierkegaard from last term, "Weren't all these thinkers anti-life with their notions of sin, renunciation, and spiritual purity?" He wondered why they would want to propose such a stance that would teach others not to value the world.

Brian Baker, another student of mine, expressed this well last spring as he closed his group's class presentation with the following comments while drinking his Coke: "Every day about this time I buy a Coke and drink it. I enjoy this Coke and consider it money well spent. None of the philosophers we've read, except Socrates himself, would understand this. They would think I should not enjoy something that is material not spiritual. They themselves would feel guilty even if they allowed me to enjoy it. This Coke gives me pleasure; it contributes to my well-being. My family has little money. We manage to keep getting jobs; most days we enjoy work and life. These philosophers do not understand this; they do not understand the ordinary world. They do not appreciate it and it shows in their philosophy." I applaud Brian's thoughtful observations and I am immediately aware that it is difficult to know where to go with them. It would be easier if Brian had said he would start giving his Coke money to those even poorer than himself or if he had talked about giving up Cokes because they were bad for his body or at least if he had promised always to recycle the aluminum soda can, and in each instance exhort the rest of us to do the same. Those claims would have the proper ring of pushing something away from the self. If they did not evoke the image of a wandering mendicant at least they would sound a familiar echo of inner-worldly asceticism.

Niebuhr thought that the ability of religion to separate us from the world was its most essential social characteristic which also spoke to the existential condition of moral agency. Niebuhr does not develop a notion of happiness *per se*, but we know something of what he thinks about happiness from his critical discussion of the liberal terms of a satisfactory life with their Enlightenment assumptions. In Enlightenment terms, happiness is obtained through the pursuit of reasoned choices which are of themselves harmonious and good. Happiness, reason, freedom, and the good are bound together as a self-defining and self-reinforcing mixture whose reflective and common sense value appear to be without question. John Rawls appeals to this legacy when he defines happiness as the successful carrying out of a rational life plan, that is, a plan whose rationality satisfies the good and makes possible the "harmonious satisfaction of his interests."[1]

Niebuhr found all of the terms bound up with the Enlightenment view of happiness highly problematic. Niebuhr called liberal morality the morality of "the easy conscience." It is in his view a morality that requires no moral effort at all. The good naturally ensued from reason; conflicts were ameliorated, and self-satisfaction emerged as the inevitable result. Religious and secular liberalism approached morality with the "easy conscience" by which reason and self-interest were without power and evil and were of themselves good. From Niebuhr's perspective liberals were too much at home in the world and too happy to be here. They had no realization of the power of individual or collective ego and thus no appropriate awareness of the power of evil.

The appropriate awareness of ego, power, and evil comes from the acknowledgement of an absolute transcendent being, God, and from the distance from the world that such an awareness makes possible. Niebuhr spoke of this distance as the "essential homelessness of the human spirit."[2] Such homelessness made possible not only a critical perspective but also supplied the only true source of meaning to human life. "For the self which stands outside itself and the world cannot find the meaning of life in itself or the world."[3] To make the world our home is to take on its conventions and calculations, to lose the criticism of the world that religion has to offer. Such renunciation would appear then to be religion's most distinctive feature. Niebuhr rejected the possibility that religion could transform the world; it is the wisdom of religious understanding that we cannot do so. He also rejected the notion that the world was so lost that it lay outside the proper realm of human responsibility. He argued that it is the social function of religion "to criticize the present."[4] Because we cannot realistically expect to transform the world, we must criticize it. Criticism then becomes an expression of renunciation. Niebuhr did not say to be unhappy when we do this, but somehow we know that that is what he meant when we read the unrelenting prose of *Moral Man and*

Immoral Society. Being realistic is not only an ironic business but also a grim business. It is not a discourse of sympathy but of scolding and punishment, and the discourse carries this implicit message whether it was Niebuhr's intent or not. (A Boston lawyer friend who had once been a graduate student in religion commented to me once that after reading Niebuhr you would not want even to give someone a cup of water. Perhaps this is one reason many of his disciples spend a lot of time defending him as a person in distinction from his written texts.)

At the same time, I am sympathetic with Niebuhr's critical task. Niebuhr feared sentimentality and naivete. He feared convention and the ways in which morality itself legitimates power and eases the consciences of the powerful. He also feared irrelevance. His argument about the need for morality to face up to the realities of power was an argument that morality needed to make contact with the world at a point at which it really matters. But politics also compromises morality and so the price for contact, however necessary, is great. Compromise saves us from tossing back and forth between complete renunciation and absolute perfection; it steers a middle course. And yet we forever pay the price because politics is something we cannot love. If we are to do it right, we must hold it at arm's length, view it with the ironic double eye, and resign ourselves to its calculations even as we struggle to press it toward justice. This version of inner-worldly asceticism quickly reminds one of Weber, who identifies, as Hannah Arendt observes, the successful venture of Protestantism and capitalism in motivating human activity with no enjoyment at all.

At the same time this expression of world-renunciation which sees politics as the consequence of sin involves a kind of cheating. Niebuhr was very much at home in the world. I would say he even enjoyed politics, that grim necessity. He enjoyed a position of relative power and he clearly enjoyed being around power. This pleasure was not simply putting the best face on resignation and alienation; it was not simply the "since I have to be here I might as well have a good time" syndrome. At the same time, the position of Christian realism announced a claim of remoteness from power in its notions of irony and ambiguity. Apparently the pleasures of politics and power are hidden even from Niebuhr himself by irony, by his claim to be a displaced person not at home in the world.

Niebuhr's theory then does not describe happiness or well-being or pleasure. This absence is problematic for several reasons. One is that he seems to enjoy the world of politics; granted, he enjoys it by virtue of being the critic. But he likes this activity; he engages it robustly. It would appear that having the kind of social power he had as a critic was a source of pleasure. This goes unacknowledged both as an uncriticized issue of Niebuhr's ego and social location and also as an unrecognized source of pleasure from this world. Fear of acknowledging one aspect may in fact engender fear of acknowledging the other. In addition, Niebuhr gets to have it both ways. He gets to enjoy the advantages of social power with which he appears to be very much at home and at the same time claim the position of homelessness. Martin Marty once commented that for all Niebuhr's criticism of it, Niebuhr could not imagine that anything other than middle-class life was desirable to anyone.

A second problem is that Niebuhr's text counsels dissatisfaction and uneasiness. The central vehicle for that alienation is the world. Yes, Niebuhr declares that the central problem is human sinfulness and the self-interested aggressive power that results. But he has framed the issues of power in such a way that the world is also blamed for not meeting the standards of individuals. As the aggregate of power, society is always less than individuals, and the more individuals are attached to society, the more they are impeded by it. We can reject the world without second thought because it fails to measure up to the notions of perfection available to the individual human imagination, notions which have been the classical source of religious and philosophical happiness.

Yet notions of world-renunciation and their accompanying notions of perfection are embodied; they are about people. Historians of religion argue that the development of renunciation as religious expression in the traditions that emerge in what Karl Jaspers called the "Axial Period" took place in response to new experiences of suffering as populations began to cluster more tightly in cities and suffer disease. Gombrich notes the appearance of renunciation in Hinduism during this same period. Without settling this issue, it is also evident that in their historical origins notions of renunciation are bound up not simply with the rejection of society but also with the renunciation of a particular group of people. That pattern continues in liberal notions that society is a lesser good. Individuality is associated with the bourgeois male. Society is associated with those who cannot slough off their relations, relations that pollute reason and freedom.

In various ways and extents, women, the poor, and peoples of color are labeled, with society, as something unfree and lesser in the values they can express and receive.

At the same time such groups can become objects of idealization, for example, the moral purity of women or the innocence of the poor. This pattern makes evident the resonance between renunciation and idealization as well as the ways this resonance reinforces power. People who are part of what is to be renounced can be idealized as the repository for feelings and desires that official notions of perfection and renunciation forbid. By locating such people in a lesser life form, that of society or the world, we can surreptitiously imbue them with what is missing in the official account while at the same time holding to the hierarchy of the official account.

Reinhold Niebuhr wanted to construct a new discourse for the moral life that would take into account the wiles of the individual ego and the serious evils that result from the ego compounded collectively. He wanted the discourse to be neither optimistic nor pessimistic but realistic. He rejected what he saw as the utopianism of liberalism and what he saw as the strict world-renunciation of Luther's view of politics. It may be difficult at the end of the twentieth century to imagine a more appropriate discourse for morality than that of Christian realism with its terms of irony, ambiguity, and paradox, with its emphasis on the dangers of illusion and the ease with which we rationalize our power, with its Sisyphus-type view of the struggle for justice.

But I think that this response frames the moral life in a way that leaves out important aspects that the question of happiness invites us to reconsider. The discourse of realism is existential and invites the image of moral activity as heroic extremity. The moral actor is homeless in this world, alienated by the necessity of participating in its power, and resigned to doing so. Morality is held in place by the ironic fit of power as domination and an absolute notion of perfection. However, all of these terms easily become absolutes. Instead of mitigating worldly power, consider the possibility that they reinforce it. It is not just that the calculation of power requires the absoluteness of perfection but also the other way around. In order to keep itself in place, absoluteness of judgment and rule requires domination.

Notions of renunciation, at least in Christianity, also place great emphasis on the will. In moral theory will translates into oppositions and adversaries. Moral positions quickly become absolute. We fear the hapless relativity that appears to be the only other alternative. Will is a notion of withholding and holding the fort against the onslaught of all that would undermine us. But then our moral "resolutions" only reproduce the opposition between what we accept and what we reject. Morality is taken to be a matter of casting off something that we no longer need to care about, just as we cast off the world. People then voice surprise that someone they disagree with "is a human being after all." This notion of moral criticism reproduces the notion of reason as an activity of detaching and separating instead of relating. This is the reason of standing outside to better see what is in there. But if moral criticism separates us from the problem, then it is also a tool of power in separating us from those we need to communicate with, and it is a tool of alienation in separating us from the very world in which moral relations are made. Finally, it is a form of domination by which our vision of perfection, whatever it may be, becomes the means for telling everyone else what they have to do. It is a perfection that is hard and never laughs.

The morality of renunciation is without sympathy for what it sees as its "object," a position one can only afford if one thinks he or she will never meet this "object" again. In doing so it neglects the morality of ordinary behavior in the ordinary world. This world is not worthy of its attention in its lack of extremity and in the more negotiated way in which problems get solved. As a consequence the ordinary activity of human beings, the dilemmas and satisfactions it brings, has trouble finding a place in a moral structure that devalues this world and pushes it away. But then we are not acknowledging the moral activity of ongoing life, whether it is an unusually helpful electrician or the kind way in which a neighborhood looks after its local eccentric. Further, we do not understand the consequences of our own behavior in the ordinary world, the daily patterns by which we interact, the micro-practices by which we use power, extend and withhold sympathy. All of this seems unimportant, expressive of a world that is only background noise, that is only there to give some of us food, clothing, and shelter. It also ignores the ways in which the familiar things of the world make us happy and in that happiness make us more generous, more flexible, and more aware of why people think their lives are worthwhile.

I have traced here what I see to be a dominant, if sometimes hidden, pattern. It is a pattern on which many terms are staked regarding the understanding of morality, of transcending experiences, of what it is to be meaningfully alive. It is not the only pattern but it is one easily associated with those of us who claim our work to be about the moral life. Niebuhr presented realism as our which maturity requires. I disagree. The suspicion of this world is too much about fear and opposition. It is too much the adolescent who defines herself against the world, who taunts her adversaries, and who fears that the world indeed is coming at her.[5]

There are reasons to be concerned about happiness. Many things make people happy that I would reject, not only by profession but as a human being. We cringe for the adolescent because we know she will be disappointed, disillusioned, because we fear what will happen to her in a world of dangers that will variously confront her depending on where she lives, the color of her skin, the contents of her parents' bank account. But surely this knowledge is not the last word. Surely, as adults we can make some distinctions with confidence between well-being and sloppy contentment so that we do not teach others to fear and disvalue the world—even as we try again and again to make the world a place in which those most vulnerable can enjoy less fear and more value.

NOTES

1. John Rawls, *A Theory of Justice* (Cambridge, Mass.: Belknap Press of Harvard University Press, 1971), pp. 63, 550.

2. Reinhold Niebuhr, *The Nature and Destiny of Man*, vol. 1 (New York: Charles Scribner's Sons, 1941), p. 14.

3. Ibid.

4. Reinhold Niebuhr, *Does Civilization Need Religion?* (New York: Macmillan Co., 1927), p. 163.

5. See James Keenan, "What's Your Worst Moral Argument?" *America*, 2 October 1993, pp. 7–10.

Happiness as the Pursuit of Meaning: The Promise of Professionalism

WILLIAM M. SULLIVAN

I. PROFESSIONALS AND THE MORAL LIFE

"THE MOST MANIFEST SIGN of wisdom," wrote Montaigne, "is a constant happiness."[1] Whatever else it means, happiness implies that a
person or a community has achieved a measure of purposeful integration and well-being. By Montaigne's standard, professional life, to
which American society looks for much of its understanding of life,
does not seem to be faring particularly well. The news media bom-
bard us with accounts of unhappy professionals amid professions in
crisis. Physicians suspect that the public has turned against them and
live in fear of oppressive regulation administered by punishing offi-
cials. The public now distrusts the legal profession, while large
numbers of young attorneys in major firms wish they had chosen another occupation. Teachers are chronically dissatisfied with their
conditions of work. Academics are attacked for everything from un-
dermining the great truths of the Western tradition to perpetrating
outrageous "profscams."

Whatever the distorting effects of sensational journalism, critical intellectual appraisals of professional life do not provide a
significantly more positive picture. Consider some recent examples.
The late Christopher Lasch described the professional mentality as a
"culture of critical discourse," particularly dominant in the university,
a culture for which nothing is holy or "exempt from reexamination,"
a critical temper predisposed toward cynicism. This is a view which
exalts competence over character, manifest in a "snobbish disdain for
people who lack formal education and work with their hands" while
it retains "an unfounded confidence in the wisdom of experts."[2] As a

counter to the nihilism of professionals, Lasch held up the heroic struggle for character extolled in the tradition of populism.

Less sweeping, but also unsettling, is Derek Bok's finding that professional compensation during the past two decades has been radically skewed toward leading figures in the private sector. Bok has pointed out that in the United States the pay and perquisites awarded leading business executives, physicians, and lawyers are two or three times greater than those earned by their peers in European nations. By contrast, professionals serving the public sector, such as teachers, civil servants, and social service providers, earn significantly less and enjoy far less social prestige in America than do their European and Japanese counterparts. Bok argued that these tendencies directly defeat the nation's long-term interest in a balanced distribution of "talent" among a variety of professional fields. As the United States funnels disproportionate rewards into a few areas of the private sector, talented young people oversubscribe those fields, to the detriment of overall social efficiency and often their own happiness.[3]

Or, consider Robert Reich's gloomy analysis of the way the global economy is changing relations between work and community loyalty. These changes are spearheaded by and most evident among professionals, higher-level managers, and the growing army of consultants of all types whom Reich collectively dubs "symbolic analysts." Taken together, symbolic analysts make up about one-fifth of the nation's work force but absorb half of all income. They are the key resource for producing high-value goods and services, the key to America's competitive position in the world economy. But Reich also fears a deep strand of nihilism in the leading professional ranks.

The culture of symbolic analysts rewards the "skeptical, curious, and creative," encouraging the carryover of techniques of "problem solving, problem identifying, and strategic brokering" into life outside of work.[4] Whatever their individual motivations, however, their position at the advancing edge of global trends in industry, research, communications, and management links these symbolic analysts into increasingly transnational networks for which notions of national loyalty, social justice, or common sacrifice are "meaningless abstractions."[5] Like Lasch, only more wistfully, Reich sees the demise of a work ethic which entails public responsibility. For Reich, however, the culprit is not simply a rationalistic and arrogant professional culture, but a global economy grown over the heads of nations and citizens alike.

What, then, of the experience of being a professional today? In *Fear of Falling: The Inner Life of the Middle Class*, Barbara Ehrenreich has provided an illuminating collective portrait of what she calls the "professional middle class." She tells a story of the rise and proliferation of this class during the years between World War II and the yuppie era of the late 1980s.[6] While noting many of the social and cultural tendencies the other critics emphasize, Ehrenreich also attempts to understand the positive features of professional life from the inside, as it were. She asks what has made professional work so sought after and, even with all its problems, deeply satisfying to so many Americans.

The answer, Ehrenreich argues, is that there are intrinsic qualities to professional work which provide middle-class professionals "a secret pleasure principle." That is, professional work is not only socially respectable. It also entails significant engagement with technically fascinating activities, collegially pursued, which provides the exhilaration of meeting manageable yet fresh challenges. Its satisfactions can be sufficiently deep to provide "an alternative to the less satisfying, and hence more addictive, hedonism of the consumer culture."[7] Professional life, then, is among possible lives one particularly conducive to an active and socially generative kind of personal happiness. This is an important claim to be revisited later.

Professionalism is thus for Ehrenreich a source of both social benefit and personal fulfillment. Under the right organizational conditions, Ehrenreich believes that the reflective engagement of trained capacities with the problems of modern complexity can be intrinsically motivating. For Ehrenreich, the chief threat to this motivation comes from the workings of the market economy. The market lures the successful into loss of commitment through the seductions of consumer culture. At the same time it puts pressure on the ambitious to trade integrity for affluence, as in the yuppie syndrome. Ehrenreich's aim is not to undermine professionalism but to strengthen its positive features by democratizing it. She urges incorporating some of the key features of professionalism, especially the autonomous exercise of expertise and dignified social standing, as standard features of all job descriptions. Ehrenreich is in effect giving new expression to a currently unfashionable tradition of liberal and left political thought, enunciated by figures such as Emile Durkheim, R. H. Tawney, and Louis Brandeis, which promoted the professionalizing of work as a key strategy for humanizing the market economy.

All four critics agree on the strategic importance of the professional groups in modern American society, and, for good or ill, the widespread influence of professional ways of thinking and living. But after this they, like much of the larger public, part company. So, which angle of vision should one adopt: the radically critical angle taken by Christopher Lasch, the humane social utilitarianism of Derek Bok, Robert Reich's morally concerned but, in the end, economically deterministic view? Or should one take up a critical but reforming perspective such as Ehrenreich's? In what follows I will try to make a case for the critical but reformist view not only as being more socially responsible, but also as enabling us to attend to more of the complexity and ambiguity of professionalism than the others. This complexity, I will argue, is important to grasp, not only to understand the professional middle class, but also because the problems faced by that class bring into clear focus the challenges posed by this difficult moment of late modernity.

II. RECONSTRUCTING PROFESSIONALISM:
A PRAGMATIC APPROACH

Reconstruction is a term of art in American pragmatist philosophy, especially as used by John Dewey. As a critical approach it seems especially apt for social and cultural questions of the sort about which no one can pretend to a totally objective standpoint but which demand serious and responsible efforts at understanding and response. As a species of practical reasoning, reconstruction is a modern descendant of the "practical philosophy" developed by Aristotle in his *Ethics* and *Politics*. Reconstruction in this practical sense is implicit in every exercise of critical intelligence. This is the core insight of pragmatist philosophy.

Reconstructive practical reason focuses on practices that have in some situations become problematic, that is, lost, confused, or self-defeating. Reconstruction proceeds by taking apart the components of the problematic situation in a new form so as to unblock the constricted or dissociated patterns of activity. Reconstruction is intelligence at work to better fulfill the purposes implicit in a certain practice by finding a more successful way of understanding or acting toward the goals of that practice, thereby realizing more fully its potentialities.[8]

Reconstruction always involves interpretation, in the sense of a construction of the situation in terms of an imputed purpose. But the truth value of the interpretation is always provisional and, in the language of contemporary social theorizing, its rationality is communicative in nature.[9] The "proof" of the validity of reconstruction is itself always a gesture of faith toward the future and has about it something of a Pascalian wager. The judgment that the defining purpose imputed to a situation has been sustained is by necessity a complex reflective process. Its most important indicator, though still a provisional one, is that the new understanding permits thinking or activity to flow in ways which restore or augment the complexity and coherence lost to the situation or activity in its formerly problematic condition.

To move from theory to a case, consider how contemporary professional life might appear from the perspective of reconstructive practical reason. We will examine a particularly troubling development in contemporary professional life, the so-called yuppie syndrome, to highlight the key problematic features of professionalism. Then we will conclude the discussion by asking, in light of the current challenges, what kind of understanding and institutionalized practices would be needed if professionals are more effectively to achieve the individual and common goods inherent in their work.[10]

Professionals take part in the commercial life of civil society. Like other workers, they make their living by trading upon their capacities in the labor market. However, professionals enter the labor market with credentials, and sometimes state-certified licenses, which establish them as the owners of a marketable type of property, a kind of human capital. This capital is the result of their development of skills and acquisition of knowledge in specialized institutions, especially the university. Like physical capital, professional capital is appropriated by individuals and negotiated in the market. In this way, the possession of professional credentials confers a measure of independence upon its possessors, giving scope to their individual potentials.

It does this in two ways. In the external sense, the professional degree or "shingle" provides for recognition. It confers upon its possessor a socially significant identity, a standing from which to advance a career "open to talent." In an internal sense, too, the professional's acquired knowledge and skill opens possibilities for finding challenges and satisfactions in applying those capacities to situations in resourceful, even innovative, ways. In other words, by possessing their peculiar form of human capital, professionals gain both dignity and opportunities for creativity, thereby enhancing and realizing the self.

The security and negotiability of the professional's human capital exists, however, only as part of the public order of civil society. Even more than most other kinds of property, professional capital depends upon civil society's structure of legal procedures and reasonings. For example, the law benefits professionals by regulating the market for their services; it protects society by defining enforceable standards of practice. Professional status is in principle open to all, regardless of social origins. Yet individuals can garner the benefits of professional credentials only by joining a corporate group defined by moral expectations as well as standards of technical competence. By becoming professionals, individuals attach their personal identity in important ways to a collective project, and find themselves held publicly accountable for the reliable performance of services according to prescribed procedures.

Entering a profession, then, does more than open up opportunity. It also makes the individual dependent upon the disciplines and control of a quasi-corporate form of life. Without this, the individual is in a far more precarious market position. In a sense, professional "property" is shared property. In order to be able to make individual use of professional capital, the individual must be licensed by a professional community. This demands of the individual a demonstration of the character as well as the expertise that defines being a doctor, lawyer, accountant, scientist, or teacher. To extend the economic metaphor, we can say that the professional's human capital can produce effects only within the network of "social capital," the expectations of competence, trustworthiness, and honesty which are generated by a community of practitioners through sustained cooperation.[11]

There is significant tension between these two features of professional life. The first feature, the freedom to employ one's human capital to maximum advantage and personal satisfaction, strains against this second feature of dependence upon a demanding, collective enterprise. Yet professional freedom of opportunity is realized only through the individual's acceptance of responsibility for the purposes and standards which define the profession. Individual initiative and collective loyalty depend mutually upon each other and yet pull in opposite directions. This tension is inherent in any interdependent situation, but it could be argued to be a particularly salient feature of modern societies based upon an extensive division of labor. That this is heightened in professional life only indicates how representative the professions are of the larger social world of modernity.

For professionals, this tension is heightened by the fact that the negotiability of professional "capital" is highly dependent upon a third, civic or public factor: the public legitimacy of professional services. These services, after all, are often beyond lay ability to understand fully or to judge. There is thus an inescapable relationship of trust between practitioner and client involved in any successful professional enterprise. In the United States this has meant both implicit civic compacts between particular professions and the public, such as exist in higher education, or the development of explicit charters of relations between public and profession in the structures of the bar, medical boards, and various kinds of certification.

The third, civic dimension of professionalism thus emerges from the fact that professional capital is so visibly a social and political artifact. In a democratic society professional legitimacy is always precarious. It can only be secured so long as a general balance is maintained between the kinds and degree of professional privilege and the public's perception that professional services contribute significantly to the public welfare. The importance of recognizing this third, civic dimension to professional life becomes apparent from the consequences of its neglect, when professionalism is viewed in abstraction from its civic context of negotiated interdependence. Then, professionals and their enterprises appear either as fixed features of society whose legitimacy is taken for granted—or as strikingly successful monopolists who have used public credulity at their self-proclaimed credentials of expertise to manipulate legislatures into granting them outrageous privileges and power. Neither view holds out either reason or hope for constructive engagement with the tensions outlined above. One either endorses whatever is, or condemns it, without responsibility.

By contrast, this effort at intellectual reconstruction has construed professionalism as a still incomplete project whose eventual outcome remains unclear. It has, however, uncovered three constituent features of professionalism: (1) professional skill is human capital that is (2) always dependent for its negotiability upon some collective enterprise which is itself (3) the outcome of civic politics in which the freedom of a group to organize for a specific purpose is balanced by the accountability of that group to publicly established goals and standards.

Through this process of reflection, professionalism's implicit aim has begun to emerge into some clarity. That aim is to organize the conditions of work so that workers can develop and express their individual powers by engaging them responsibly in ways that assure the individual recognition through contributing to enterprises of public value. This purpose links expertise, technical innovation, and freedom of enterprise to individual fulfillment through the responsible discharge of socially recognized tasks.

By its inherent logic professionalism addresses a central problem of modern life. This is the question of meaning, much discussed in some circles today. Meaning refers to the sense of value people experience when they understand their own lives to be linked in a significant way with the larger processes at work around them. It has both an inner and a public face. To discover meaning is to find a point to living by recognizing oneself as a participant in a worthwhile enterprise whose accomplishment calls out one's energies and whose purposes define and vindicate one's having lived.

To live with meaning is to have discovered the secret of happiness. In the modern world, the sources of meaning are plural, a significant advance over the narrow possibilities offered to most persons in traditional societies. This is in part the result of the extension of freedom to ever greater sectors of the population, enabling women, the young, and ethnic and racial minorities to begin defining their own lives. Meaning, then, can lie not only in work but in family life, religion, friendship, the arts, knowledge, national and global concerns.

In modern societies with a highly differentiated yet relatively open division of labor, work plays a key role. Work provides the means by which individuals can develop their capacities and express their individuality when also experiencing the solidarity attendant upon shared goals and values. The value of professional life resides in its having served as a collective experiment, or series of experiments, in devising an answer to the question of how meaning can be institutionalized in work.

III. THE CHALLENGE OF THE UNHAPPY
PROFESSIONAL CONSCIOUSNESS

The upshot of our reconstruction of professionalism is that its defining purpose is to unite the social benefits of applying technical expertise to affairs with the search for meaning in the world of work. These goals indicate the civic nature of professionalism. Professional life ought to be an ideal place in which to cultivate a modern, diversified kind of citizenship through vocational commitments that provide both public values and self-realization. But as the critics of professionalism surveyed at the outset remind us, this is far from being the usual case. Nevertheless, the worth of this exercise in intellectual reconstruction will be demonstrated if it enables us more clearly to assess what is wrong and, at the same time, begin to formulate a more adequate response to the situation than has been available.

Realizing the potentials of professionalism, like all other purposes, has to be worked out in the face of historical contingency, manifest in the state of economic development, the institutional order, and the tendencies in the sphere of culture. The interests of the critics surveyed fall out roughly along these three vectors. Robert Reich's analysis suggested that the workings of the global economic order are not favorable to the realization of professionalism among "symbolic analysts," while Derek Bok showed how the United States was in the process of institutionalizing a version of professional life hostile to civic responsibility. Christopher Lasch emphasized the corrosive effects of a relentlessly skeptical and instrumental form of thinking which he thought was sweeping all before it.

All three analyses portray a contemporary setting of unhappy consciousness in which public and private purposes have become increasingly disjoined. The economic context is one in which the storms of "creative destruction" sweeping the world commercial system are swamping most of the institutional dikes constructed around and within national economies. Firms, workers, regions, and finally individual professionals are being forced into a more desperate competitive game in which winners become fewer as the stakes get higher. Culturally, the instrumental and utilitarian outlook does not appear to be anchored in any institutional loyalties which might either limit its workings or give it point. The result is the rise in professional life of the cultivation of detached competence, a gamesmanship which, in a competitive pinch, easily goes over into irresponsible opportunism and exploitation. These tendencies make it harder to respond to an increasingly anarchic global and domestic situation. This hardly seems a good context for the development of the professional and civic virtues which would be needed to build up bonds of social trust in order to reverse these entropic tendencies.

The yuppie syndrome is perhaps the most compressed—and disturbing—exemplification of these tendencies. The lives of the young urban professionals first noted as a social phenomenon in the boom years of the 1980s present a crystallized model of the contemporary dilemma. The yuppie confounds much of our conventional cultural wisdom. Contrary to the supposed contradiction between a sturdy work ethic and the hedonistic aims of modern consumerism, such as that presented in Daniel Bell's *The Cultural Contradictions of Capitalism*, the yuppie both works very ambitiously and has an insatiable appetite for the consumption of stimulating commodities and experiences. The problem of the yuppie life is rather that both success and pleasure seem, as Barbara Ehrenreich pointed out, not only precarious but ultimately capricious and vain.

The institutional context of yuppie life is, despite material security, riven by harsh dichotomies. Competence and adaptability are the presiding values in work and all public activity. Competence, while much valorized, is strangely abstract, with few ties to particular ends or life-structuring commitments. The demands and stresses of highly competitive work are expected to be balanced or at least relieved in the intimate realm of personality. Yet "relationships," including marriage and family, are sources of enormous concern and, often, severe disappointment.

Simply trying to manage the conflicting demands of a highly segmented life requires a complex strategy for keeping it all going and, finally, soothing the wounds of the self. Hence, yuppie life is marked by a considerable consumption of professional services, from child care to financial planning to psychotherapy, all of which tend further to fragment existence, threatening to turn the art of living into a grim struggle for psychic survival.

This dichotomy between the harsh demands for competence in the marketplace versus the softer private sphere of personality is familiar to broad groups in modern society. It is rooted in the often sharp differentiation between the public and private spheres. Our economic, political, and administrative institutions have become increasingly governed by instrumental and utilitarian norms, so that as workers and professionals we must focus upon technical competence. In our other capacities, however, as consumers, citizens, members of associations, a different logic often applies, in which the expression and fulfillment of individual wants become paramount.[12]

At work, that is to say, many of us become "Weberians," bent on rationalizing activities, while in the recesses of private life we are "Bloomsburies." There, when we believe that we can truly "be ourselves," we often find ourselves emulating that privileged Edwardian set who, no longer finding meaning in the public values of their era, sought redemption in the cultivation of an autumnal hedonism, a romanticism tinged with terminal irony. Modern persons, even postmodernists, must compromise between these ideal typical lives, leading sometimes a Weberian, now and again a Bloomsbury, existence. This division of life into contrasting spheres of value was what Max Weber himself thought of as the fate of modernity. Earlier, it had seemed to Hegel the manifestation of alienation, a state of unhappy consciousness at war with itself.

The material basis for this development in the United States was the organization of a stable yet enormously dynamic consumer economy following World War II. This twenty-five-year-long "American Century" of world predominance, economic growth, and expansion of personal freedom was also the period in which the professional ranks grew into a fifth of the work force. The fundamental principle of that era, which has set the terms of life for the remainder of the century, was well expressed in the adage that "a rising tide lifts all boats." It was believed that "growth," abstractly measured as economic expansion, was the solution to all social problems. It was an approach that fit with a national tradition of weak public institutions and a strong spirit of private enterprise. However, it ensured that while professionalization expanded widely, its directing values would often veer toward the instrumental rather than the civic.[13]

The purpose implicitly animating the American strategy was an individualistic, Lockean liberal conception of the public sphere. In this understanding, which has a long history in American society, the public sphere is an arena in which autonomous individuals freely bargain and contract with one another on the utilitarian basis of an enlightened self-interest. This American growth strategy contrasted strongly with the development of the European and Japanese economies during the same period. There the national state led public efforts to reduce inequality and support negotiation and mutual accommodation among classes and groups. Especially in the social democratic countries such as Germany and those in Scandinavia, the growth of the professions concentrated upon public management of social problems such as health, urban expansion, and education, as well as in the development of a highly skilled work force. Focused upon such public purposes, these nations went a considerable distance toward extending the features of professional work to most occupations, including ongoing training, initiative, and long-term security.

What was overlooked in the American "growth society" model was the dependence of its individual agents, its human capital, upon the factor of "social capital," the moral matrices of community life and cooperative association. To avoid consuming this social subsoil, the growth society would have had to attend to the ties of interdependence, actively seeking to nourish the civic tendencies within all areas of social life, including the professional realm. It in fact did relatively little in these directions.

More recently, the increasingly violent oscillations in economic boom and bust have intensified the pressures toward instrumentalizing all relationships. As we have seen, this has made commitments to public values, and therefore the essential moral infrastructure of civilized freedom, harder to sustain. Among the more secure, the result has been varying degrees of involvement in the yuppie syndrome. But among the urban poor, as Cornel West has recently shown, the result has been a far more immediately destructive nihilism.[14]

The error of the leaders who managed the postwar "consensus politics" was their belief that change could be accommodated without involving intellectual or moral challenge for the citizenry. For several decades under the double aegis of Cold War and managerial expertise, the cooperation of big business and big labor with government regulated the national economy to produce the most dynamic yet institutionally stable economic growth the United States has ever known. As the scale of the world economy grew, however, American business, the senior partner in the relationship, saw its interests diverging more and more from those of the bounded national economy. Under increasingly fierce global competition, American multinational and transnational business and finance pulled out of the social contract in the 1970s, setting off the increasingly intense competitive antagonism and political near-gridlock. This is the historical context for the analyses of professional imbalances proposed by Robert Reich and Derek Bok.

This kind of increasingly desperate, unregulated competition is not good for any society. Neither is it likely to be economically sustainable. As a logic of action it is seriously misconceived. There has been a slow breakdown of that system of economic regulation which did a fair job of managing competition to maximize its long-term benefits to the whole. This breakdown has set every social interest off on a suspicion-driven strategy based upon the old logical fallacy of competition. That is the error of assuming that, in an interdependent system, what is good for each individual participant—in this case all-out competitive striving—will produce benefits for the whole. On the contrary, the result of the widespread adoption of that strategy has been the decline of social trust and a concomitant rebounding of the self-protective aggression of the competitors upon their own heads. Its greatest negative consequence, however, has been to weaken confidence in the possibilities of cooperation. Yet only cooperation on a new scale can render competition constructive and enable us to avoid the grim prospect of increasingly vicious zero-sum confrontations.

In the economic realm that self-destructive syndrome became familiar in the era of the Great Depression. Then firms, seeking to lower their costs and thereby shore up their own economic position, shed workers in vast numbers. The effect, of course, was collectively ruinous, for what lightened the costs of individual firms also collectively depressed the purchasing power of the market for their goods. The governmental management of the national economy which sustained postwar growth was the institutional solution which grew up in response to the problem—against, it should be noted, the violent protests of many of the individual firms who were thereby rescued from oblivion. In the social realm, a similar effect is observable. In American cities, fear and distrust due to spreading crime and perceptions of threat from strangers have set in motion a defensive spiral of withdrawal from common life. As a result, the bonds of mutual assistance among citizens and between citizens and their government, upon which the security of each depended, have been increasingly frayed. The resulting situation virtually forces each individual to look to private security or flight as the only response. To date, no effective solution has been developed for this problem.

In both the economic and the social cases, the parties involved suffer from the effects of what we could call negative interdependence. Interdependence turns negative in its outcomes when it is inescapable, yet neither acknowledged nor taken as a shared responsibility by those involved. The result is social entropy, with seriously negative consequences for the individuals through the collapse of the social environment upon which they depend. In even the moderately long run, no purely individual solution can overcome the underlying logic of interdependence. Either the individuals learn to cooperate, regulating and sharing responsibility for the collective effects of their actions, or they continue to suffer the downward spiral of negative interdependence. As the political struggles of the Depression era demonstrated, it has often been difficult for Americans to recognize this. Today we face a similar but greater challenge to our social capacity to reflect and innovate, a challenge both more socially profound and vastly greater in scope.

The alternative to such entropic outcomes is positive interdependence. The outcome of interdependence becomes positive where the interacting parties develop the breadth of understanding, skills of cooperation, and willingness to share responsibility for collective endeavors which enable them to turn the situation to their advantage. They learn to increase the complexity, flexibility, and stability of their environment rather than depleting it. These characteristics restate the classic civic virtues, as the social practices of cooperation and mutual responsibility describe the practical bases of a vital civic culture.

An environment of positive interdependence proposes more to individuals than just opportunities for private fulfillment in exchange for onerous discipline at work. Rather, such societies hold out the possibility of a more expansive life, including a more expansive sense of self, as the intrinsic rewards of self-disciplined civic commitment. As historical evidence suggests, dynamic civic orders can liberate their citizens to become more than they at first wished or imagined. Many professionals, even amid the stresses of this anarchic economic period, experience through their vocational commitments the stimulation and the satisfaction which modern civic life can afford. This is their "secret pleasure principle."

IV. THE PRACTICAL SIGNIFICANCE
OF PROFESSIONALISM

The emerging global economy needs new transnational structures of cooperation, which are today still embryonic at best. That is the source of much human suffering and demoralization, for the affluent, as we have seen, but even more miserably for the poor. The only way out on this increasingly tight little planet is not by escape but by engagement, through developing capacities for positive interdependence. It seems more and more clear that national societies will fail or prosper precisely as their citizens prove able to invent new and timely forms of civic life. This is the context which heightens the significance of professionalism. As we have seen, professionalism is a civic institution of cooperation planted within the workings of economic life. Its vital mission is to hold up the need to infuse economic life with opportunities for individuals to develop themselves through contributing to public values. At its best, professional life models this aim in practice.

In this quest, the professional project can benefit from the intellectual resources offered by pragmatist philosophy. For pragmatism teaches that the contingencies of history are not entirely the work of transhuman forces. To a significant extent, human problems are of human making, chiefly the results of faulty, one-sided institutional design. But what has been made and proved wanting can, with skill and luck, sometimes be remade for the better. This philosophical hopefulness, which often strikes citizens of the Old World as wildly naive, is no doubt due in considerable measure to the United States' comparatively fortunate national experience. What pragmatism needs in order to be relevant now is not so much tempering by the tragic as a dose of sociological realism. In short, pragmatists need to take institutions and their deep effects upon human character more seriously.

As the enduring patterns of interaction through which human beings live, institutions are the most omnipresent and powerful of educators. A society focused upon the market teaches its youth effective lessons about the need to get ahead and the disgrace of failure. Societies with strong central states inculcate a sense of the majesty of the collective will, making public service, even self-sacrifice for the nation, accepted and common outcomes. Institutions can do these things because they structure attention and, if they are coherent and vital, provide rewarding reinforcement in the attitudes appropriate for their purposes.[15]

Institutions are the entering wedge by which moral meaning shapes technical and instrumental functions. They "moralize" merely instrumental functions by embedding them in networks of moral expectations.[16] They are generators of social capital, resources of trust upon which individuals can draw as they pursue their own purposes and to which they contribute by practicing their occupations in responsible ways. Thanks to institutions, the tasks of getting a living or solving social problems or figuring out how to live together can become foci for enriching character, friendship, and self-transcending loyalty.

Professionalism, as a form of civic life, can give moral significance to the instrumental functions of work in ways which allow its participants to control and take responsibility for their actions as free persons. In this way, the aims of professionalism, understood in their full, public scope, can significantly advance the cause of democratic reconstruction to which pragmatist philosophy has also been historically committed.

Institutions, then, are tangible bearers of meaning, carriers of causes, vehicles of common life. In the theological language of H. Richard Niebuhr, they are also loci of faith.[17] As a uniquely modern institutional form, professionalism can be a bearer of hope for greater wholeness in an alienating time. Its secret is simply that professionals are able to take part in activities which are intrinsically meaningful for themselves and valuable contributions to the cause of the larger human community.

As opposed to much contemporary opinion, our investigation suggests that the key to personal happiness is not having our desires met. The key is, rather, having an objective, practical activity in which our capacities are stirred by challenges neither overwhelming nor too easy and our energies are focused outward upon enriching the world. A happy life is one spent perfecting practices which cohere in meaningful ways. But it is the forms of institutional life which ultimately control the kind of challenges we will meet and their manageability. Thus, the institutional patterns in which we live, and the practices which they permit and support, are the most important determinants of the happiness and meaningfulness of our lives.[18] To pursue happiness, to seek meaning, require taking seriously a civic responsibility to sustain and reconstruct the institutional order of democracy.

This is the promise of professional life. Anyone who has been stirred and inspired by a committed teacher, an attentive health care provider, a dedicated pastor or rabbi, or who has worked in or been served by a well-functioning firm, agency, school, church, or even university, has glimpsed the human possibilities inherent in communities of professional purpose. These glimpses raise a question that is at once philosophical, theological, and practical: Why not live so as to make this purpose our own? But that, perhaps, is a topic for a further exploration.

NOTES

1. Michel de Montaigne, "On the Education of Children," in *Essays*, trans. J. M. Cohen (London and New York: Penguin Books, 1958), p. 67.

2. See Christopher Lasch, *The True and Only Heaven: Progress and Its Critics* (New York: W. W. Norton, 1991), p. 530.

3. See Derek Bok, *The Cost of Talent: How Executives and Professionals Are Paid and How It Affects America* (New York: Free Press, 1993).

4. Robert B. Reich, *The Work of Nations: Preparing Ourselves for Twenty-First Century Capitalism* (New York: Alfred Knopf, 1991), p. 230.

5. Ibid., p. 309.

6. See Barbara Ehrenreich, *Fear of Falling: The Inner Life of the Middle Class* (New York: Pantheon Books, 1989).

7. Ibid., pp. 13, 15.

8. See John Dewey, *Reconstruction in Philosophy*, enl. ed. (Boston: Beacon Press, 1957), esp pp. 26–27 and 51ff. See also Robert C. Neville, *Reconstruction of Thinking* (Albany: State University of New York Press, 1981). The following discussion also draws upon the contemporary development of Deweyan practical reasoning by Charles W. Anderson, *Pragmatic Liberalism* (Chicago: University of Chicago Press, 1989) and *Prescribing the Life of the Mind: An Essay on the Purpose of the University and the Cultivation of Practical Reason* (Madison, Wis.: University of Wisconsin Press, 1993), esp. pp. 11–23.

9. The notion of the "rational reconstruction" is basic to Jürgen Habermas's theory of communicative action. See *The Theory of Communicative Action*, vol. 1, *Reason and the Rationalization of Society*, trans. Thomas McCarthy (Boston: Beacon Press, 1984), esp. pp. 220ff.

10. The following discussion draws heavily upon my analysis of professional work provided in William M. Sullivan, *Work and Integrity: The Crisis and Promise of Professionalism in America* (New York: Harper Collins, 1995).

11. The notion of "human capital" has come to play an important role in contemporary social research in highlighting the practical significance of shared expectations and moral ties. For an explication of the concept, see James S. Coleman, *Foundations of Social Theory* (Cambridge, Mass.: Harvard University Press, 1990), pp. 300–321.

12. These are the key themes of what is called American individualism. See Robert N. Bellah, Richard Madsen, William M. Sullivan, Ann Swidler, and Steven M. Tipton, *Habits of the Heart: Individualism and Commitment in American Life* (Berkeley and Los Angeles: University of California Press, 1985).

13. These developments are described and analyzed in more detail in Robert N. Bellah, Richard Madsen, William M. Sullivan, Ann Swidler, and Steven M. Tipton, *The Good Society* (New York: Alfred Knopf, 1991).

14. See Cornel West, "Nihilism in Black America," *Dissent* (Spring 1991), p. 221–26.

15. For elaboration of these ideas, see Bellah et al., *The Good Society*, esp. pp. 1–18, 287–304.

16. See Philip Selznick, who has developed a rich theory of institutions on pragmatist lines, in *The Moral Commonwealth: Social Theory and the Promise of Community* (Berkeley and Los Angeles: University of California Press, 1992). The argument of this book has informed my own in this section.

17. H. Richard Niebuhr, *Faith on Earth: An Inquiry into the Structure of Human Faith* (New Haven, Conn.: Yale University Press, 1989), p. 51.

18. These themes, broadly pragmatist and Hegelian in inspiration, are the organizing ideas of Lawrence Haworth's *Decadence and Objectivity* (Toronto: University of Toronto Press, 1977), esp. pp. 83ff. Haworth's arguments receive empirical confirmation in the psychological research of Mihaly Csikszentmihalyi, *The Evolving Self: A Psychology for the Third Millennium* (New York: Harper Collins, 1993).

Will the Cubs and Red Sox Ever Meet Again? Playfulness and Happiness

JAMES R. LANGFORD

THE YEAR WAS 1918 and World War I was soon to reach its stalemate and then head toward an armistice. Still, before the 1918 season, the Red Sox had to replace twelve men, including the manager, who entered the armed forces. For all of the justifiable criticism to be leveled at him in later years, Sox owner Harry Frazee did well in signing or trading for replacements. Led by pitcher, outfielder, and first baseman Babe Ruth, the Red Sox held the league lead long enough to earn a World Series berth against the Chicago Cubs. It was a strange season in every way. The owners agreed among themselves to close the season early—some five weeks early. Though they used the war effort as an excuse, it was a major decline in attendance that lay behind their action. In 80 per cent of a normal season, attendance was down 40 per cent from the previous year. The owners simply stopped play, gave all players ten days notice (thus saving the remainder of the payroll), made all players free agents, and agreed among themselves not to tamper with anyone else's players. Who says you can't have your cake and eat it too?

Lament: Oh, if only some similar collusion had taken place to stop the season before September 10, 1969, Chicago's Cubs and not the Miracle Mets would have ruled that year!

Observation: Greed, the lack of a Commissioner, collusion by owners in 1918, the Black Sox scandal a year later . . . was there ever an innocent age for America's sport?

The greed that shortened the season in 1918 cast a shadow over the World Series too. The first three games were played in Chicago, but not at Cubs Park—later to be known as Wrigley Field. The Cubs in effect gave up their home field advantage by choosing to use Comiskey Park, home of the American League White Sox, in order to have more seats to sell.

In Game 1, Babe Ruth outpitched Hippo Vaughn 1–0. Vaughn is legendary in the hearts of Cubs fans: on May 2, 1917, he pitched a no-hit game for nine innings only to lose 1–0 in the tenth to the Reds' Fred Toney, who pitched a no-hitter through all ten innings. It is germane to note that Toney was an ex-Cub. The Cubs won game 2, 3–1, and sent Hardluck Hippo Vaughn back to the mound in Game 3. He lost 2–1 when the Cubs second baseman tried to steal home with two out in the ninth, a move not even Don Zimmer would have been able to countenance.

Then came the train ride to Boston and an encore for the Babe. This time he beat the Cubs 3–2. Attendance at the first four games had totalled less than 90,000. Someone told the players that the owners had earlier decided to take 30 per cent of the players' pool to distribute to the second-, third-, and fourth-place finishers in each league. Both teams saw the handwriting on the wall and resolved not to play another game until there was a guarantee of $1,500 for each player on the winning team and $1,000 for each member of the losing team. The strike ended only when Mayor "Honey Fitz" Fitzgerald made an emotional speech from home plate announcing that the game would be played for the sake of the wounded veterans in attendance. Hippo Vaughn won 3–0 on a five-hitter. A day later, Carl Mays of the Red Sox pitched a 2–1 win and the Series was over. Some months later, Sox owner Harry Frazee sold Babe Ruth to the Yankees for $125,000 and made a kind of Cub comment: "I believe the sale of Ruth will ultimately strengthen the team." It sure strengthened the Yankees!

Now that's a nice story about the last time the Red Sox were world champions, but who cares and what does it have to do with happiness?

Baseball may not be a metaphor for life but I think it teaches many lessons and embodies many truths that are valuable in pursuing a good life and a happy life. I submit that playfulness—whether it be about something as ephemeral as a sports contest or as serious as death—is a *sine qua non* of happiness.

My philosophical position is, with no apologies, Aristotelian, particularly Aristotle as understood, commented upon, and sometimes appropriated, by Thomas Aquinas. For Aristotle, Augustine, Aquinas, and, in fact, a large contingent of Western philosophers, the ultimate end or goal of a human person is happiness. Everyone desires the complete good, but not all agree in what that complete good consists. Some regard wealth or sensual pleasure, honors, fame, or power as that good, as their ultimate concern.

Aquinas comments: "It is impossible for complete human happiness to consist in a created good, for happiness is the perfect good which wholly brings desire to rest, for it would not be an ultimate end if something should remain to be desired. Now the object of the will or human appetite, is the universal good, just as the object of the intellect is universal truth. Hence it is obvious that nothing can bring the human will to rest except the universal good. This is not found in any created thing, but only in God, for all creatures have goodness by perception. Hence, only God can satisfy the human will."[1]

That sounds very much like an echo of Augustine's "You have made us for yourself and our hearts are restless until they find their rest in you."[2]

Now that very assertion that perfect human happiness can be found only in knowing God is at the heart of a cosmic drama. To know God by tracing visible effects back to the first cause is a limited degree of knowledge, but it is all the human intellect, left to itself, can attain. Christian theologians have had always to contend with the frustrating fact that humans have a goal they can't reach without help. Pelagius and his followers argued that this was an uneven playing field and that human actions therefore must be able, by themselves, to get a hook into supernatural grace so that we could reach our ultimate goal by the power of our own acts. Christian theology rejects that view in favor of the gratuity of grace as a gift from God that enables humans to attain their goal. This has enormous implications. The description of a good and happy human provided by an atheistic humanist and that advanced by a Christian humanist might well be identical except that the latter requires the paradoxical twist that to be completely human, one needs the gift of supernatural grace. Fallibility has more than a foothold. The Cubs and Red Sox are not anomalies at all.

Aristotle reasoned that since the mind is the greatest of human faculties, happiness will be found more properly in a life of thought than in a life of activity and in an act of reason more than in the act of an appetitive power controlled by reason.

He says in the *Nicomachean Ethics* that it is proper for a good person to act well according to reason, and for the very good person, or happy person, to do this in superlative fashion. The happiness attainable in this life must extend to a complete life; one clear day does not prove that spring is here, and one good deed is not enough to make a person good—or happy.

Thus it is that moral virtues as habits of good action according to reason are what engage a person for a happy life. They are the repeated practices of good action that free the mind to contemplate. To live a happy life means to steer a course between excess and defect. *In medio stat virtus.* Between foolhardiness and cowardice lies fortitude. In the use of money, between vulgar display and meanness is magnificence; between extravagance and stinginess lies liberality. The extremes are vices, bad habits; the mean is where the virtues are found.

Nearly every facet of human life has activities that can be carried to extremes or conducted according to reason. And the point is that the virtues all work together to foster happiness in a person. It is not enough to know virtue; one must practice it. Virtue facilitates happiness, which, in turn, motivates virtue.

Since the human condition does not allow for uninterrupted intellectual contemplation, and since everyone needs some relaxation from the anxiety and stress of living, Aristotle saw the value and need to posit a virtue to guide us in the practice of amusement. It is the virtue of *eutrapelia*, "playfulness" or "wittiness," and it stands between the excesses of the buffoon on the one hand, and the dour lout on the other. Aristotle says that "people who engage in too much derision are buffoons and nuisances wanting laughter at any cost: on the other hand, persons who say nothing funny and are disagreeable to those who do, seem uncultured and rude" (*Nicomachean Ethics* 1128a–79).

There is something in human nature that marks risibility as more than an accessory. Even in the most dire situations, people find a way to smile, laugh, or mimic. There are stories from the Nazis' concentration camps of prisoners entertaining each other by imitating the strut of the guards.

W. C. Fields' remark "On the whole, I'd rather be in Philadelphia" is the legacy of a laugh in the face of death. And we know that the most successful comedians are those whose material is the stuff of everyday life.

My fascination with baseball is not only aesthetic and athletic; it is with the individual and collective narratives that comprise its history.

I don't know whether anyone can explain completely why any one franchise rather than another claims his or her allegiance and affection. In my case, I know it was not genetic; my father, sister, and brother all cheered for the Chicago White Sox. At the age of eleven I started to follow every Cubs game. They were mostly played in the afternoon in those days and I would race home from school and tune in Bert Wilson on WIND radio. Bert was an incredible optimist and a salesman without peer. George Will has described how the Cubs of the late forties made him into a conservative—how, after finding improbable ways to lose game after game, the Cubs taught him to expect the worst and to be suspicious of any claims that changes would make things better.

The whole thing had an opposite effect on me. I became a liberal; I rooted for the underdog. The preseason odds were always the same: Cubs to win the pennant, 100–1; the World Series, 500–1. I cheered our band of rightly unheralded rookies and over-the-hill veterans against the Dodgers and Giants with their big-name stars and superior attitude. That meant buying into absurdity. That meant stacking up, say, our catcher Harry Chiti, who weighed more than he hit and who the Cubs organization heralded as the "new Gabby Hartnett," against the likes of Roy Campanella and Wes Westrum. Chiti, as one Cub fan said, "looked like everyone's brother-in-law. And played like him, too."

Never mind. I learned early that winning isn't everything. And in those days, I could reason that the Law of Averages was simply trying to catch up with the Cubs who had won ten pennants between 1900 and 1945. Never mind either that they lost eight of the World Series they played in. As if teenage life is not troublesome enough, I had to try to understand how the Braves could win a pennant with Spahn and Sain and two days of rain but the Cubs couldn't with Kush and Rush and two days of slush.

Over time, I learned the truth of Aristotle's contention that happiness is not found in power. In the early '50s the Cubs had slow-footed home-run hitters named Kiner and Sauer in their outfield, and all they did was wear out poor Frankie Baumholtz who was sentenced to play center field between them. Happiness is not found in fame either. Some of the most famous stars in baseball have been acquired by the Cubs after their arms had gone dead and their bats had fallen silent: Dizzy Dean, Robin Roberts, Jimmy Foxx, Bobby Thomson, Al Dark, Ralph Kiner, . . . the list goes on.

And there are some little-known facts that bolster Aristotle's conclusion that happiness *does* depend on the rightness of reason. In

1935 the Cubs refused a chance to pay $25,000 for a young outfielder from the San Francisco Seals of the old Pacific Coast League. Their scouting report said he had a bad knee. The Yankees took the risk and acquired Joe DiMaggio. Years later the Cubs could have had a kid pitcher named Sandy Koufax for $25,000 but they didn't want to make room on the roster for him for two years. A young star named Joe Torre would have signed but he wanted a car. For the price of a Chevy, the Cubs lost him. And the Cubs even had the inside track on Carl Yazstremski; but the front office said that they had signed Ron Santo and didn't need another third baseman, especially one that would cost $100,000! In 1964, the Cubs traded a young outfielder named Lou Brock to the Cardinals for a sore-armed Ernie Broglio. Brock went on to a Hall-of-Fame career; Broglio was working for a beer distributor in California in three years.

Over the years, I have come to regard the Cubs not as lovable losers but as Sisyphus *redivivus*, Sisyphus in the flesh. And, though not an American League fan, I could not help noticing a similar story being written by the Red Sox.

I defected from the National League to root for the Red Sox against the Mets in the 1986 World Series. The Mets had no ex-Cubs on their roster and the Red Sox had only one—Bill Buckner. A fine hitter and decent fielder, a man who played in pain for years with an ankle that made him run like Long John Silver, poor Bill Buckner made the error that allowed the Mets to win. It is worth noting that the Red Sox gained some measure of payback to the Cubs by trading Al Nipper and Calvin Schiraldi (who together were 0–3 in the World Series) to Chicago for Lee Smith. Chicago writers warned the apartment dwellers across the street in left field to put screens over their windows in anticipation of Nipper's arrival at Wrigley.

Now in my fifth decade as a Cub fan, I cherish the hope this allegiance has nourished; the pleasure, relaxation and happiness baseball has provided me. But most of all, I treasure the wit and wisdom that serve as almost daily reminders of the human condition and the need to smile and push on. For me, Cubs baseball is General Manager Jim Gallagher saying of the 1948 Cubs, "This was the best team ever to finish last in the National League." It is shortstop Len Merullo making four errors in one inning and naming his son, born that day, "Boots." It is the honesty of pitcher Dave Cole when told the Cubs had traded him to the Phillies. "That's too bad"; he said, "they're the only team I can beat." In fact two of his three wins the year before were over the

Phillies. It is Cub great Ernie Banks saying, "If you aren't happy one place, chances are you won't be happy any place." It is Cubs leader Bob Kennedy saying of the Brock-for-Broglio deal, "I think this is going to make us more respected."

Cubs baseball is a politically incorrect pitcher named Moe Drabowsky who made it to the World Series as an Oriole. "I was the second Pole to appear in the World Series," he said. "The first one carried a rake." It is manager Charlie Grimm in 1948 sending scouts across the land to find someone to help the Cubs' hopeless offense. A scout wired: "Spotted a pitcher who stopped a good team cold. Only one ball was hit out of the infield and that was a foul fly." Grimm wired back: "Forget the pitcher. Send the guy who hit the foul." Cubs baseball is relief pitcher Bill Caudill explaining a bad outing: "Even Betty Crocker burns a cake once in a while." Cubs baseball was the big tension on the 1966 team as to which Cub hitter would lead the league in strikeouts. What a finish: Adolfo Phillips and Byron Brown each fanned 133 times! It is manager Joe McCarthy's maxim: "Don't alibi on the bad hops; anyone can field the easy ones." It is manager Frankie Frisch's advice to new managers: "Stay away from firearms and don't room higher than the second floor." It is ex-Cubs player Chuck Tanner musing, "You can have money stacked to the ceiling, but the size of your funeral will still depend on the weather." It is manager Preston Gomez resigning slightly more than halfway into his first season, with the comment, "If I had known *then* what I know *now*, I would never have taken this job." It is being within seven outs of going to the World Series in 1984 only to lose the playoffs to the surfing San Diego Padres.

Cubs baseball is to go fifty years since a pennant and then have people say that the last pennant, in 1945, was bogus because the teams were depleted by the war. How many times do we have to hear sportswriter Warren Brown's response to the question, "who will win the '45 series, the Tigers or the Cubs?" "I don't think either team can win" was his answer.

As recently as last season, the Cubs listened to and paid a phrenologist who said he could predict the future careers of players by the shape of their head. "Hang on to pitcher Jim Bullinger," he advised. And the beat goes on.

Cubs baseball is Milt Pappas, one pitch away from a perfect game, watching umpire Bruce Froemming call, "Ball four." Froemming said later, "How could I sleep at night if I called that a strike?" To which Pappas replied, "If that's the case, you wonder how he ever sleeps."

It is oversized catcher Hector Villanueva musing, "When I'm hitting, they say I'm stocky; when I'm not, they say I'm fat." Cubs baseball is coming back from a 21–9 deficit against the Phillies only to lose 23–22.

Cubs baseball is Cubs manager Don Zimmer on being roundly booed for leaving a pitcher in too long, "For a minute there I thought I was back in Boston."

For me Cubs baseball is a kid listening to Bert Wilson and believing that the game is never over until the last man is out. It is going to Wrigley Field with his grandfather and remembering forty years later where he sat and what he saw.

It is wishing with every bit of his heart that he might have played—if only for one out—as a Cub. It is believing, and hoping, and enjoying, in ways non-Cubs fans cannot understand. Cubs baseball is always to love the game, if not the result; always to savor the sights, if not the score. It is to feel an unspoken alliance with any stranger whose bumper sticker reads, "Go CUBS!"

Will the Cubs and Red Sox ever meet again and play the Series at those two monuments where legends played and myths began— Fenway and Wrigley? If they do, I for one will be looking to the sky for the Messiah along about the seventh inning of the seventh game. I hope the score is tied and the game is called on account of happiness.

NOTES

1. Thomas Aquinas, *Summa Theologiae*, Ia–Iae, q. 2, a. 8.
2. St. Augustine, *Confessions*, Book 1, Section 1.

Author Index

Subject Index